The Wonderful World
of Words

Marsteller

The Wonderful World of Words

Memoranda and Speeches
of Bill Marsteller 1951–1972

Table of Contents

Table of Contents

An Introduction to Bill Marsteller

by Melvin Anshen
Professor, Graduate School of Business,
Columbia University

One day in the spring of 1956 a stranger named Bill Marsteller invited me to lunch at the Duquesne Club in Pittsburgh. He wanted to talk about the possibility of my consulting from time to time on management problems of the advertising and public relations business he had launched a few years earlier. The company was still rather small, but it was growing and prospering and his eye was on its future.

After years of experience in journalism and marketing management, Bill had started the business in 1951 as an industrial advertising agency with offices in Chicago and Pittsburgh. Within a couple of years a public relations affiliate was established. Two years later the firm acquired an industrial agency in New York City. By 1972 the operations of Marsteller Inc. were conducted through offices in New York, Chicago, Pittsburgh, Los Angeles, and Washington in the United States; Toronto, Canada; and across the Atlantic in London, Brussels, Geneva, Stockholm, Stuttgart, and Paris. From its initial concentration on serving clients selling to industrial and agricultural markets, the scope had expanded to consumer products and services, medical products, financial public relations, and counseling on corporate policy. Converting its total revenues to conventional billing terms, operations in 1972 aggregated a business of about $100 million. And Bill Marsteller's eye is still on the future.

My first sharp impression on meeting Bill was of a man who knew exactly where he meant to go and how he meant

to get there. Above all else, he wanted to produce communications programs embodying advertising and public relations of outstanding creative quality. He did not cherish this goal for aesthetic reasons or to win awards. In his view, truly creative communications programs were those that worked effectively and efficiently to build markets, sales, and profits for clients. He was confident that such programs would also satisfy aesthetic criteria. But the real test was to achieve planned communications objectives within clients' marketing programs. This is still his belief and his creative commitment.

He wanted to produce results-oriented communications in a special kind of organization that reflected the professional and personal ideas and values evolved through his career. Such an organization would accomplish more than the superficial success of profitable growth. He wanted to build and lead a business of this character not only for the pleasure he would find in the experience, but also because he was confident that talented people working in this environment would create advertising and public relations of unusual power to serve clients' needs.

Long before Ted Levitt announced his seminal management planning question—"What business are we in?"—Bill had the root concept clearly in his mind. The business he was in was the creation of total communications with all publics. By "total communications" he meant not only the traditional external communications of advertising and public relations, but also communications within client organizations for administrative, educational, and informational purposes. By "all publics" he meant not only customers and potential customers, but also all other groups within and outside a client's business. And since he thought that no rational businessman should spend his communications budget without measurement of results and payback on investment, his concept of the business included an in-house capability for performing marketing and communications research.

To assure the professional integrity of the service of each

client's account, Bill designed and personally supervised a creative quality control system with twin objectives. The first was to stimulate an unending drive for creative excellence in all advertising and public relations materials. The second was to assure that no mediocre or careless work could leave a Marsteller office. The system included a written communications plan for each account, with built-in provisions for measuring performance against goals established with client agreement; creative planning and review for work-in-process; annual critiques of creative performance in each office; and annual stewardship reports to clients on performance against planned objectives. Beyond the formal control system there was always Bill Marsteller reading the ads and public relations documents and reacting to the brilliant and the dull with messages that reminded account executives, writers, and artists—and market researchers, media specialists, and production managers, too, where their contributions counted—that the Chairman of the Board was a man who knew and loved his craft and wanted every associate to know and love it in the same way, to respect only excellence, and to despise all work of lower quality.

His principles of excellence of creative output, dedication to clients' objectives, and loyalty to associates have built enduring relationships. On the twentieth anniversary of the firm's foundation, he recalled with pride that two of the agency's largest clients in 1971 had been the two original clients of the business. Most of his earliest associates are still members of the management team.

Bill Marsteller's commitment to the highest standards of professional performance in the creation of communications programs is matched by an equal commitment to professionalism in the management of his business. In his view, effective internal administration gives clients more return for their investment in communications while also increasing agency profits. He believes that an advertising and public relations agency should be a planned and controlled business, not a cottage industry or an arts-and-crafts shop. He

thinks it should be managed as well as the most successful client companies, using all the tools and techniques of modern administration. It should have analytically selected long-range objectives of scope and sizes and profits; a set of designed strategies for achieving these goals; a continuing planning function for appraising progress and amending goals and strategies as appropriate; and a realistic system of short-term budgets for controlling financial and other operations. The information system should promptly identify variances from standards and illuminate their causes as a basis for prompt correction. His concept has called for administration through multiple profit centers and detailed profit-and-loss analyses of individual accounts. Consistent with these information requirements, Marsteller Inc. was the first agency of its size and one of the first of any size to invest in a computer. It has been a leader in using the computer for management purposes, as well as for routine accounting and billing assignments.

Bill believes that clients' interests and employees' knowledge and confidence are equally benefited by clear written statements of fundamental policies. Everyone knows the score in this business because the score is in writing and performance is recorded and evaluated. Some employees of the agency may, on occasion, have found some policies irksome, but they observe that Bill lives by them no less thoroughly than he expects others to do. He thinks it demeans no one to sign in and out, least of all himself. He believes that creative talent is in no way discouraged or constrained by written communications plans, prudent use of clients' money, orderly offices, and universal courtesy in human relations.

Bill believes in creating opportunities for people to work at the peak of their abilities and be rewarded for their accomplishments. The company operates through multiple profit centers partly to put decision making close to problems and opportunities, but partly also to provide the gratifications of general managerships for numerous associates. He believes, too, in the growth of professional skills and in

personal development for all. This belief translates into performance evaluations that lead to written plans for personal growth, in-house training programs and management seminars, and company-sponsored attendance at outside career-related courses.

Believing as he does in the value to clients of well-designed advertising and public relations programs, he thinks this view is equally relevant for his own business. Throughout its history Marsteller Inc. has spent a larger share of its gross income on advertising and promoting its own services than any other agency.

No significant measure of his commitment to professionalism in management is the presence of "outside" directors on the Marsteller board—three out of eight in 1971. In departing from the common agency practice of filling board seats with full-time executives, Bill has sought two gains from the presence of outsiders. The first is objective, independent appraisal of top management performance, including his own. The second is fresh ideas from minds unencumbered by operating details. He sees no distinction between the value of outside directors in client companies and their value in his own business.

While Bill's core attention has never wavered from the performance of the agency bearing his name, he has also given energy and vision to outside interests. He has been a discerning collector of works of art which are displayed in his homes and in company offices. He has contributed counsel and support to the University of Illinois, his alma mater, and to Barnard College where he serves as trustee. By personal service and through his encouragement to his executives to serve, he has strengthened professional associations in the communications industry.

Above all, he has coached and stimulated young people in all ranks, taking pride in their performance and advancement in the business. To all of them working with him, while rarely an easy and relaxing experience, has been unendingly exciting and rewarding. He is one of those rare persons whose accomplishments become a standard of ex-

cellence in the minds of others. Some of us remember the occasion when the head of one of the country's largest agencies hired a Marsteller alumnus for an important management job. Meeting the agency head not long after, Bill remarked that he was surprised that he had not been asked for an appraisal of the man's abilities. "I didn't need one," was the answer. "He worked for you for four years and that was recommendation enough for me."

* * *

Because he is a superb communicator of his ideas in spoken and written form—and because he expects no greater loyalty from his associates than he returns to them— Bill has gathered and held a management group that shares by conviction his beliefs and works together with unusual mutual confidence and trust. His closest associates in the past two decades, members of his board of directors, for their own instruction and pleasure and for the instruction and pleasure of employees of Marsteller Inc., and of Bill's other professional associates and his clients and his friends outside the business, have brought together in this volume a selection from his internal memoranda and speeches to outside audiences. We hope in this way to recall and share the unique quality, the flavor, and the bite of his mind and personality. He believes powerfully in words. He loves their precise selection and adroit placement. He uses them with sensitivity and skill. Here are some samples from his work.

Memoranda to Everyone

Bill Marsteller believes in wide-open lines of communication, up, down, and sideways, throughout the agency. He did his share to set an example for his associates over the years in a series of memoranda "To Everybody." Written when the spirit moved him, about whatever interested him, the memoranda covered a broad range of topics both great and small. They dealt with policies and operations, with creativity and communications, and with the values and attitudes and behavior of people—at once the greatest asset and the greatest liability of a personal service business.

Memoranda and Speeches
of Bill Marsteller 1951–1972
Selected by
The Board of Directors
Marsteller Inc.

*The Wonderful World
of Words*

Marsteller

Creativity

Bill Marsteller profoundly respects and values creative communications. He distinguishes clearly between creative pretensions and creative accomplishment. Out of his respect and his skepticism he has developed ideas about the genesis of creativity and the care and feeding of creative people, and shared his ideas in memoranda to his associates. Having started his own career as writer and journalist, he uses words with a superb craftsman's skill, as exemplified in the opening memorandum on "The Wonderful World of Words"—a creative statement that deserves to be anthologized.

1

TO: Everyone

FROM: Wm. A. Marsteller

SUBJECT: The Wonderful World of Words

Human beings come in all sizes, a variety of colors, in different ages, and with unique, complex and changing personalities.

So do words.

There are tall, skinny words and short, fat ones, and strong ones and weak ones, and boy words and girl words and so on.

For instance, title, lattice, latitude, lily, tattle, Illinois and intellect are all lean and lanky. While these words get their height partly out of "t's" and "l's" and "i's", other words are tall and skinny without a lot of ascenders and descenders. Take, for example, Abraham, peninsula and ellipsis, all tall.

Here are some nice short-fat words: hog, yogurt, bomb, pot, bonbon, acne, plump, sop and slobber.

Sometimes a word gets its size from what it means, but of course sometimes it's just how the word sounds. Acne is a short-fat word even though pimple, with which it is associated, is a puny word.

There's a difference between tall-skinny words and puny words. Totter is out-and-out puny, while teeter is more just slender. Tea, tepid, stool and weary are puny.

3

Puny words are not the same as feminine words. Feminine words are such as tissue, slipper, cute, squeamish, peek, flutter, gauze and cumulus. Masculine words are like bourbon, rupture, oak, cartel, steak and socks. Words can mean the same thing and be of the opposite sex. Naked is masculine, but nude is feminine.

Sex isn't always a clear-cut, yes-or-no thing on upper Madison Avenue or Division Street, and there are words like that, too. On a fencing team, for instance, a man may compete with a sabre and that is definitely a masculine word. Because it is also a sword of sorts, an épée is also a boy word, but you know how it is with épées.

Just as feminine words are not necessarily puny words, masculine words are not necessarily muscular. Muscular words are thrust, earth, girder, ingot, cask, Leo, ale, bulldozer, sledge and thug. Fullback is very muscular; quarterback is masculine but not especially muscular.

Words have colors, too. To wit:

Red: fire, passion, explode, smash, murder, rape, lightning, attack.
Green: moss, brook, cool, comfort, meander, solitude, hammock.
Black: glower, agitate, funeral, dictator, anarchy, thunder, tomb, somber, cloak.
Beige: unctuous, abstruse, surrender, clerk, conform, observe, float.

San Francisco is a red city, Cleveland is beige, Asheville is green and Buffalo is black.

Shout is red, persuade is green, rave is black and listen is beige.

Oklahoma is brown, Florida is yellow, Virginia is light blue and Massachusetts is dark green, almost black. Although they were all Red, Khrushchev was red-red, Castro orange, Mao Tse-tung gray and Kadar black as hate.

One of the more useful characteristics of words is their age.

There's youth in go, pancake, hamburger, bat, ball, frog,

4

air, surprise, morning and tickle. Middle age brings abrupt, moderate, agree, shade, stroll and uncertain. Fragile, lavender, astringent, acerbic, fern, velvet, lace, worn and Packard are old. There never was a young Packard, not even the touring car.

Mostly, religion is old. Prayer, vespers, choir, Joshua, Judges, Ruth and cathedral are all old. Once, temple was older than cathedral and it still is in some parts of the world, but in the United States, temple is now fairly young. Rocker is younger than it used to be, too.

Saturday, the seventh day of the week, is young while Sunday, the first day of the week, is old. Night is old, and so although more old people die in the hours of the morning just before the dawn, we call that part of the morning, incorrectly, night.

Some words are worried and some radiate disgusting self-confidence. Pill, ulcer, twitch, itch, stomach and peek are all worried words. Confident, smug words are like proud, lavish, major, divine, stare, dare, ignore, demand. Suburb used to be a smug word and still is in some parts of the country, but not so much around New York any more. Brooklyn, by the way, is a confident word and everyone knows the Bronx is a worried word. Joe is confident; Horace is worried.

Now about shapes.

For round products, round companies or round ideas use dot, bob, melon, loquacious, hock, bubble and bald. Square words are, for instance, box, cramp, sunk, block and even ankle. Ohio is round but Iowa, a similar word, is square but not as square as Nebraska. The roundest city, is of course, Oslo.

Some words are clearly oblong. Obscure is oblong (it is also beige) and so are platter and meditation (which is also middle-aged). Lavish, which as we say is self-confident, is also oblong. The most oblong lake is Ontario, even more than Michigan, which is also surprisingly muscular for an oblong, though of course not nearly as strong as Huron, which is more stocky. Lake Pontchartrain is almost a

straight line. Lake Como is round and very short and fat. Lake Erie is worried.

Some words are shaped like Rorschach ink blots. Like drool, plot, mediocre, involvement, liquid, amoeba and phlegm.

At first blush (which is young), fast words seem to come from a common stem (which is puny). For example, dash, flash, bash and brash are all fast words. However, ash, hash and gnash are all slow. Flush is changing. It used to be slow, somewhat like sluice, but it is getting faster. Both are wet words, as is Flushing, which is really quite dry compared to New Caanan, which sounds drier but is much wetter. Wilkinsburg, as you would expect, is dry, square, old and light gray. But back to motion.

Raid, rocket, piccolo, hound, bee and rob are fast words. Guard, drizzle, lard, cow, sloth, muck and damp are slow words. Fast words are often young and slow words old, but not always. Hamburger is young but slow, especially when uncooked. Astringent is old but fast. Black is old, and yellow—nearly opposite on the spectrum—is young, but orange and brown are are nearly next to each other and orange is just as young as yellow while brown is only middle-aged. Further, purple, though darker than lavender, is not as old; however, it is much slower than violet, which is extremely fast.

Because it's darker, purple is often softer than lavender, even though it is younger. Lavender is actually a rather hard word. Not as hard as rock, edge, point, corner, jaw, trooper, frigid or trumpet, but hard nevertheless. Lamb, lip, thud, sofa, fuzz, stuff, froth and madam are soft. Although they are the same thing, timpani are harder than kettle drums, partly because drum is a soft word (it is also fat and slow) and as pots and pans go, kettle is one of the softer.

Sometimes word images are too complex to put into rigid categories. They simply come through as a whole idea.

For instance, many people have talked about Batten,

6

Barton, Durstine and Osborn being like a trunk bouncing down a flight of stairs. Ogilvy & Mather is like tea time at a tweedy tailor's. Ruder & Finn is like mice running in the kitchen when you turn on the lights. Ketchum, MacLeod & Grove is vegetable-beef soup with barley. Hill & Knowlton is a beautifully-printed house organ that nobody reads but many people save. G. M. Basford is an old Pullman car with stale cigar smoke. N. W. Ayer is an Episcopalian prayer. J. Walter Thompson is a man getting his picture taken between Charles Evans Hughes and William Howard Taft. Interpublic, Inc., is a chain of turnpike toilets.

There is a point to all of this.

Ours is a business of imagination. We are employed to make faceless companies personable, to make useful products desirable, to clarify ideas, to create friendships in the mass for our employers.

We have great power to do these things. We have power through art and photography and graphics and typography and all the visual elements that are part of the finished advertisement or the published publicity release.

And these are great powers. Often it is true that one picture is worth ten thousand words.

But not necessarily worth one word.

The right word.

October 26, 1965

TO: Everyone

FROM: Wm. A. Marsteller

SUBJECT: The Climate of Creativity

Some of our management types have spent restless hours lately wondering if we have established the right climate for creativity.

This is nice. I like to see management types worry because as long as they trouble themselves with this kind of self-doubt the Company has a promising future.

On the other hand I have some opinions of my own on what constitutes a creative climate and how you go about producing creative rainfall. I was planning to address this communication to our Operating Committee, but it occurs to me that they might not agree with me in which case the gifted among you might be denied the satisfaction of saying, "It is I he is writing about." So I carry my case to the citizens.

First, from Page 1 of Meteorology I, we find that if you drill wells in the desert, or if you seed cloudless skies, you get no water.

It's the same with creativity. You don't fill unimaginative and undermotivated people with cleverness and a drive for achievement by hocus-pocus with the working conditions. Bright lights don't make bright people.

It takes more than a forked stick and a confident manner to get steady work as a rainmaker. But because thirsty people get desperate, all kind of fakers get temporary employment. If they are eccentric and wear black capes and long hair and smell faintly of Monday's buttermilk, their moment of success may be hastened, for who among us is to separate the uncalculated trappings of genius from the neurotic adornments of self-deceit?

The salaried branches of creativity are infested with the same kind of transient quacks—men and women who have convinced themselves they are creative because they want to be. And for awhile they are able to convince others by repeating out loud, over and over, "I am creative, I am creative, I am creative," all the while picking their noses in public to prove their disdain for convention.

Give the person who is fundamentally noncreative any climate you wish and you will not beget usable creation; give the pseudocreative person the climate of his own devising and he will reward you with a slow trickle of mean-

derings in derivative irrelevance, along with a steady flow of abuse.

These types, who come and go in the creative craft, building a list of credits for someone else's work, are not really a part of the problem. The challenge is to take the people who are creative, with either an active or latent sense of usable invention, and to give them the atmosphere in which to flourish. To stimulate them. To encourage them. To reward them. To comfort and keep them.

But how? What common conditions, what combinations of thunderheads and sunshine produce the climate of creativity?

For Ernie Pyle it was a battlefield, for Somerset Maugham it was the luxury of the Riviera, for Winston Churchill the quiet and austerity of his booklined study, for Jimmy Breslin it was the clamorous city room of a metropolitan newspaper. John O'Hara, a very wealthy man, worked as long and as routine a daily schedule as an insurance clerk despite the fact that he never needed to earn another dollar.

There are those who say that in advertising and public relations creativity is lost because of deadlines and because of the volume of work to be done. Yet Mr. E. Buchwald's cousin, Arthur, is creative against deadlines from which extensions are not granted, as have been hundreds of great reporters and columnists before him. I have a friend who has taught composition in a college of music for many years. Every term students ask him for additional time to submit their major work of the semester. He says that never once has a superior work been submitted after the original deadline; all the good stuff comes in on time. It is the student who has nothing to say, musically, who needs the extra time to say it.

Abe Burrows' fame as a play doctor comes from his ability to create under extraordinary pressure, but James Thurber turned out a prodigious flow of material with no apparent pressure at all.

A few years ago the five most creative advertising men then in practice were probably Bill Bernbach, Fax Cone, George Gribben, Leo Burnett and Rosser Reeves, since they are the only inhabitants of the Copywriters Hall of Fame. In the offices they occupy, the way they dress, their ability to speak in public, in their political convictions, they differ widely.

What these five peers really have in common is a compulsion to create and a willingness to work hard at it. They have not needed a certain kind of office, certain time of the day, a phase of the moon, soft music, sharp pencils, three martinis or a light covering of dandruff in order to be inventive. Their fame is rooted in their ability to be fresh and interesting and relevant and original over a long period of time for a wide variety of purposes.

Dr. Donald W. Taylor of Yale, who is one of the three or four psychological researchers who have made scientific studies in the field of creativity, finds the same thing about Nobel prize winners, whom he has investigated in depth. He has found that the temperament, education, physical characteristics, philosophical viewpoints and living and working conditions of these greatest of inventive geniuses were of as many patterns as there were people. The climate of creativity which nurtured them all was a purely personal one.

So, at last, it is my conclusion that we cannot artificially impose a climate that will be automatically hospitable to all creative people.

We can and should recognize work which is truly creative, single it out for praise and reward, and seek constantly to stretch harder for more that is unique. We can, in short, *want* creativity, and wanting it very badly we shall get more of it.

But at the same time, we cannot extinguish creative drive from those of our people who are genuinely creative. Creative people are self-driven, neither pushed nor towed. Their need for expression comes from within; their need for achievement can only be self-satisfied; their need to do

something better and different than anyone else has ever done is the creative climate that motivates them best.

March 4, 1963

TO: Everyone

FROM: Wm. A. Marsteller

SUBJECT: Confessions of a Reformed Cliché Addict

I was only 17 when I realized I had become a cliché addict.

It was nearly 13 years later before I had kicked the habit, as an old cliché-user would put it. It was a wonderful feeling, finally, to realize that I could prepare a cliché and then leave it sitting there, unused, or better yet to simply throw it out.

Cliché specialists say there are many ways to get hooked and it was my misfortune to become addicted in the most habit-forming way of all—on the sports desk of a small town daily newspaper.

In the fall, the Maroon behemoths crushed the Tiger eleven, the Cardinal gridders throttled the Lions' scatbacks, the Blue-and-White field general exploded through the invaders' forward wall, and the stubborn Maize defenders finally succumbed in a fourth chukker avalanche of aerials from the rapier-like thrusts of Flipper Flannigan, a starboard flinger.

With colder weather we moved our cliché pots indoors. Now it was the turn of the Tiger bucket squad to get revenge on the Maroon quintet, but the Cardinals were again supreme on the hardwoods, while Blue-and-White eked out a win in a cliffhanger, and Flipper Flannigan made a baker's dozen charity tosses with nary a miss to lead his mates to an upset of the Maize in a court donnybrook.

11

Among the oldsters, the big thing was the narrow margin the Pilsner kegglers enjoyed in their race for a third straight loop title, a margin they held by virtue of a shower of maple in the final frame in the third fortnight of the annual race.

Spring breezes brought out the thinlies. Now the Maroons leapt to victory through their prowess in the field events, the Cardinals ground out a triumph over the Lions in routine fashion, the Blue-and-White mile quartet, with a blazing final furlong, brought home the banner which, under azure April skies, hung limp on the staff since no breeze stirred to cast doubt on the records which fell like matchsticks. Under ideal conditions, therefore, Flipper Flannigan heaved the spear to an eyepopping new league mark.

Then the Maroon nine blew a three-run edge in the ninth with a duo of miscues and a trio of bobbles and the Tigers gathered up the marbles. Flipper Flannigan, now a moundsman, hurled a no-hitter while he whiffed an even octet of batsmen and gave up only a back-to-back pair of free passes and at the wicket, stroked a two-bagger and a full-house blast to the sun field pews to sew up his own contest.

Well anyway—

We thought it was pretty colorful writing.

In our naivete we didn't realize that it was obtuse, childish, strained, evasive, foolish, but most of all, utterly, utterly boring.

Now like most reformed, I am a reformer. I am disturbed about the uncontrolled use of clichés by my fellow man, especially those fellow men who emit public relations and advertising from our several premises.

As a starter, let's look at news releases on promotions (up, down and vertically). I have held out 11 such releases in the last couple of weeks that included these phrases in the first paragraph: "has been named," and "according to," or worse yet, "according to an announcement by."

In my current collection are five news releases with "is

12

a leading manufacturer of" and four "is available from." Mind you, this is the output of only a couple of weeks.

Nor are the advertising gentlemen any better, although they sometimes restrain themselves until the last paragraph or final frame and then cut out in an orgy of clichés that makes up for the earlier virginal copy. You are almost always urged to "write today for more information," or some variation thereof. One of the worst of the variants is to start that last collar-clutching paragraph with a question: "Want more information?"

Another finial that delights a cliché expert is "Contact your _____ dealer today." This suggests the following telephone conversation:

Reader: "Hello, are you my _____ dealer?"
Dealer: "Yes."
Reader: "I wish to contact you today."
Dealer: "You some kind of queer?"

There are more—many more—established last paragraph clichés for advertising and opening and mid-body clichés, too, but time is short and we urge you to come in today, bring a typical problem of your own for a free demonstration of how you, too, can eliminate rejects. No obligation.

It is just as easy—perhaps easier—to get hooked on visual clichés. Sometimes one wonders what hath Doyle, Dane and Bernbach wrought. Not all single page ads must be divided in two parts; not all spreads must ask the question on the left and answer it on the right; not all photographs must be stark; not all layouts must be derivative. Not all type must be sans-serif, just because it is "new." As soon as the "new" is copied slavishly, rather than imaginatively, it is immediately "old."

This is a wonderful business. Unlike many which are perpetual clichés, this business gives you opportunity for infinite originality. Once you have mastered the basic rules of your form of communication you find that you can experiment, vary, improve, to the limit of your own creative ability and ambition.

It is because of this that this business is never dull unless the practitioner is dull to start with.

August 4, 1967

TO: Everyone

FROM: Wm. A. Marsteller

SUBJECT: I'm Afraid I Don't Understand You
(And Maybe I Don't Even Want To)

There is a widely held theory that the new technologies in instantaneous international communications will bring universal understanding and peace in our time.

I wished I believed this. If it is true, then those of us who make our living as self-licensed experts in the arts of communications, will be the saviors of the world. The facts, I fear, are that the new satellite systems and other marvelous transmittal developments may only prove how little anyone really knows about the communication of understanding.

For example, there's a good likelihood that a fair number of our clients and prospects think differently than we do about what the word "communications" means.

In trying to define what our advertising agency believes is its Unique Selling Proposition, we say we are in the business of Total Communications. That would amuse Western Union, or NBC, or the *Chicago Tribune,* since we send no wires, broadcast no television programs and print no newspapers. But compared to a lot of other advertising agencies we do a much wider range of communications chores, so we go about the land selling our skills at Total Communications, perhaps confusing everyone but ourselves.

That's a nice little lesson in one of the biggest barriers you and I have to effective communications—assuming other people understand what you are talking about simply because it is so clear to you.

14

So many things get in the way of communications, and so many of them are so deeply rooted and so indelibly a part of our individual character that it is almost impossible to divorce one's self from the impediments to understanding. Some are simple to recognize but some are as subtle as the virus structure of the common cold, but equally widespread.

Let's start with language, one of the more simple blocks to communication. If I speak English and you speak French, you do not understand me, unless you are bilingual. But even if you are an English-speaking Frenchman, you may understand my words yet miss my point entirely. Take the famous Volkswagen ad which was headed "Lemon." One of my French friends who speaks quite good English could make no sense of it, and in fact the idea simply doesn't translate into French because there is no environmental framework for the idea that an inferior product is a "lemon," and indeed for the concept that any manufacturer would admit that he occasionally produced a bad product, even if he caught it before it was sold.

Last year, we were working with IBM World Trade developing a new campaign that was to run world-wide in 16 languages. We were trying to find a way to say that IBM's problem-solving capabilities were equally available in all these countries in which advertising was to run, and indeed that the kinds of problems to which the computers were adaptable were omnipresent.

We came up with a common theme—"Problems Know No Nationality." To our surprise, we found that the word "nationality" doesn't translate uniformly at all, and that what we were saying was subject to many interpretations, not all favorable. We finally settled on "Problems Know No Boundaries," which is less precise in English but more nearly what we were trying to say in other languages.

More than one fine sales proposition has run into trouble when the language changes. I am told that the powerful Avis "No. 2" program, while it translates, doesn't work in some countries where there is no traditional sympathy for the underdog, a trait of character so universally held in

15

America that the point Avis was trying to make comes across to nearly all of us with the same shade of meaning.

Even within the same language are all kinds of hidden turns.

Some years ago the head of a large English advertising agency came to visit me. He brought out a notebook in which, to save our time, he had written a series of questions about our Company, but first he said, "Some of these questions are a bit cheeky, and I have no doubt that in some cases you will want to say that it is none of my business. Please do, in any such instance, and I will quite understand and not be offended."

I told him I was prepared to be perfectly frank and that he need feel no reticence.

His first question was, "What is your turnover?"

Well, I explained to him that I understood why he would ask that first, what with all the publicity given to the high turnover of American advertising agencies. However, I explained, we were proud of the fact that ours was so small at that time that it simply made no sense to bother to keep formal records on it, and so I was simply unable to answer.

He said, "Well, if you have such a small turnover, how do you operate a business of this apparent size?"

Well, you have to be modest in a situation like that, so I said, "Oh, no one thing. A lot of things, really."

And he said, "You know, old chap, I don't mean to pry, and as I said first off, I understand that you may wish to tell me to mind my own bloody business!"

I told him that wasn't it at all; I simply didn't know. To ease the tension, I said to him, "Mr. Fielding, what is *your* turnover?"

"Twelve million pounds," he answered.

And suddenly I remembered having read that in England sales are stated as turnover.

There are so many traps. I know an American company that set up a Canadian subsidiary a few years ago. They'd read a good deal about anti-American feeling in Canada, so they obscured the American parentage in the subsidiary

name, rechristened the products and began advertising. Their advertising people, to save time and expense, simply picked up the copy intact from U. S. advertising and were surprised when they got two letters asking what U. S. company they were representing, since it was clear the promotion was originating below the border inasmuch as "flavor" and "savor" were both spelled without the "u."

Even in more homogeneous groups there are so many impediments to understanding. All of you have seen the word list test where you are asked to write down the first word you think of that most nearly associates in your mind with the test word. (Table: chair. Red: green.) Have you ever taken one with your wife or husband and compared your answers? How can two people live together for twenty-five years, apparently in communication with one another, and have less than a fifty per cent correlation?

In pre-testing advertising we run into these differences constantly. Bring fifty housewives together, show them a series of TV commercials, and ask them to play back to you what they understood the commercials to say. If you wrote the commercial, content in the belief that you have been simple, convincing, perhaps amusing, you are likely to be very distressed at the results. It sometimes seems impossible that the message could have strayed so far.

And if you think it is explained by the fact that these are emotional women, our research shows that the risks are just as great with machine tool advertising aimed at presumably logical engineers.

Yet, easy as it is to overlook these communications barriers, they are the relatively more simple ones to deal with.

The common pre-test is the best way and it can take many forms. A pilot study before the market research questionnaire is sent out broadcast. Rehearsal of your sales presentations before a small group of your own people to get their reactions. Feedback studies of advertising and public relations, to find out what understanding the audience plays back.

Once upon a time, if I wrote or said something that was

17

misunderstood, I used to argue about what I was trying to say. Now I just give up and try to say it differently. I'd rather argue about what I believe than what I mean.

Actually, the biggest obstruction to true communication is what we believe. The interpreters at Hollybush could change the language but they couldn't change beliefs. Hospitality, cordiality and wine can change the atmosphere without rooting out old beliefs. The incredible generosity of our foreign aid program may have prevented revolutions, and as a compassionate measure in a starving world it may be justified, but there is little evidence that it has had much success in changing beliefs.

Even with people you know well there may be a barricade of belief.

At the start of World War II, I was involved in personnel work at a non-union manufacturing plant in the Northern Indiana steelmaking area. It was a relatively small company and I knew everyone who worked there. I played golf in the plant golf league. I drank beer with the machinists and welders and forge shop men in the local saloons, because I liked them. I went to their Polish, Italian and Greek weddings, and was called upon to say a few words as "a friend of the groom."

Then one day the massive wave of the United Steelworkers, CIO, reached our plant door and, after a couple of inconclusive elections, we had a union. Suddenly I was sitting on the other side of a bargaining table, and suddenly I realized that underneath it all they didn't quite trust me. That was why they had a union; at some point their basic beliefs about capital and labor filtered conviction out of our communications.

So many little things get us in trouble. Perhaps you remember the sad story of misunderstanding between Eastman Kodak Company and the Rochester, N. Y. black community. It is reported that at a key point in the discussions, when it looked like things were pretty well worked out and the black leaders seemed to be convinced of Eastman's

good faith, an Eastman official started out, "You boys . . ."

Such an easy mistake! The president of the National Association of Manufacturers could say it to his Board of Directors and they would never notice it, much less revolt. But to a people with a deep resentment of having the bossman address them as "boy" even if they were seventy, it was an affront of tragic dimensions, and meaningful communications ended.

Another thing that gets in the way of communications is authorship. I've seen a test in which a statement on economics was given to a group of union members and they were asked if they agreed with it. The statement was signed George Meany, President of the AFL-CIO, and over 75 per cent of the union members said they agreed. The same statement was given to the same size group of members from the same union only this time it was attributed to Roger Blough, Chairman of U. S. Steel. This time over 70 per cent disagreed.

Then there are selfish barriers to communication, best described by these statements:

"This is the way *I* see it."

"I know what interests *me.*"

An awful lot of corporate or institutional advertising ends up a near total waste because of this approach. The way you see it is rarely the way the other fellow sees it, especially if you are the seller and he is the buyer, because you're standing at a different angle in the first place. What interests you most often interests your prospects least. Every advertising and public relations man has had the problem of trying to dissuade a client from running a picture of his new plant with all his 25-year employees in front, and a row of his products across the bottom. The word "Quality" will be prominent in the headline.

It's interesting about "quality." It is one of a group of words that is almost useless in real communication. They are worn out, and they meld into the crowd of words and you don't notice them. "Rugged" construction. What does it

mean? "Extra" strength. You pass them by in everyone else's ads, yet so many writers of advertising and PR sprinkle them through their own copy.

All of this may sound negative and pessimistic, but of course we're constantly learning more about communicating understanding.

We're learning the power of words. We know more about using the basic drives and self-interests of the audience. We are becoming better at picking a posture—of modesty, on the one hand, or authority, on the other—for consistency of impact. We're learning the value of testing, the trial balloon, and rehearsal.

While words—and of course pictures, which have character and mood too—are extremely useful, they are tools but not the craft itself.

The craft is harder to describe. Much of it is intuitive, as for instance when to be modest and when to be authoritative. The Avis campaign is a classic case of using a modest approach to disarm the audience and make it receptive for the real message. The message is not that Avis is second, of course. The message Avis is communicating is that you'll get a cleaner, better-serviced car with less waiting. Advertisers are not often modest—in fact most people are not really very modest when talking about themselves—and there is somehow an air of believability and trust in modesty if it seems genuine.

On the other hand, matter-of-fact authority has its place, too. I have a friend, a research man who is well-known and respected for the work he has done on magazine readership. Once, in a speech before a group of normally cynical agency media people, he said, among other things, that readership of trade and technical papers did not drop off in the summertime. One of the audience challenged him. "On what authority do you make that statement?" Although my friend had at that time done no real research on the subject and had no proof, he said, "On my own authority." To his surprise his questioner sat down and everyone accepted the statement as fact. In the same vein, when General

Eisenhower was president, students of his press conferences noted that he was rarely heckled on military matters, on which he was sometimes out of date, but was often questioned quite skeptically concerning domestic matters, on which he was often very well prepared.

One of the techniques that becomes a part of the craft of communication is simply reporting. Called by fancier, more saleable names, it is sometimes described as an Attitude Audit or Audience Appraisal. It is nothing more than asking penetrating questions of the customers and prospects for a product, a company or an industry and finding out what they now know, what they want to know—what turns them on or off. This is then laid alongside what the company or industry wants to say about itself. Whether there is meaningful communication depends upon whether the two can be made compatible.

Then, of course, there are the basic human drives all of which aid or impede communication. Perfume is a form of communication. Bacon cooking communicates. The Playboy bunnies, wiggling their cotton tails, communicate. The trick is to be aware of all the senses and all the routes of communication to the images of the senses.

There is no better way to find out if you have communicated than to ask someone to play back to you what you have said or written. Good advertising is usually checked in this way. George Gallup has parlayed poll-taking into a big business of reporting advertising impact.

Good sales presentations should be tested, too.

We are dedicated to the principle that all presentations should be rehearsed before a live and critical audience. If you are going to make a sales call, make it first in your office and develop an atmosphere which encourages your associates to be critical of each other. Don't worry about form or manners; worry about whether your point is getting across. Do other people understand you? When the man says "I'm afraid I don't understand you," he is also saying under his breath, "And maybe I don't even want to."

When you come right down to it, the art of communica-

tions is the ability, which positively can be cultivated, of automatically thinking in terms of the audience instead of yourself. It is the ultimately instinctive habit of telling me what you are going to do for me, before you ask me to do anything at all for you. It is the ability to be genuinely interested in other people and other people's interests.

It is, in short, the art of selflessness.

December 1, 1970

TO: Everyone

FROM: Wm. A. Marsteller

SUBJECT: What To Do On Saturday Morning

We have made arrangements for you to attend the finest seminar on creative communications ever presented in the United States by giving you Saturday mornings off. All you have to do is get up before nine o'clock and turn your television set to the educational channel in your city.

The seminar is called SESAME STREET. Originally planned for preschool age audiences, its inspiration comes from the much-abused art form, the television commercial. By now it has repaid its debt and some of our best new television commercials are based on SESAME STREET techniques.

There is a popular belief that advertising and public relations are businesses for the young. I have never accepted that, or at least not since I became the only person left who regards me as young. I think they are businesses for the sensitive, for the incurably curious, for people who are totally intolerant of boredom.

It isn't always easy to keep an open ear, an open eye, an open mind and an open heart as the years go by. So new experiences have to be built into the diet of the creative communications man and woman.

22

For that purpose I commend SESAME STREET to you as a substitute for almost anything you may be doing on Saturday morning. Big Bird, Bert, Ernie, Gordon, Susan and even Oscar the Grouch will be your friends, and I don't find too many friendly people abroad on Saturday mornings.

Lest some wisenheimer point out that the SESAME STREET seminar is also operative on weekday mornings, I should explain that we have been unable to make arrangements for you to stay home to watch it then.

September 29, 1969

TO: Everyone

FROM: Wm. A. Marsteller

SUBJECT: These Are Our Problems

We have just conducted our annual creative review of all domestic advertising from all offices and individual comments have been submitted on a great many accounts to the General Managers.

There are some general observations, though, that I'd like to share with you. While these observations are specifically related to advertising, it seems to me that almost universally they apply to a lot of the feature stories and major PR work that I have examined lately fully as much as they do to the ads.

Our biggest problems seem to be these:

1. We sometimes forget there's a reader or viewer out there and in a great many cases we write to the clients' interests or our own. Self-oriented ads, like self-oriented people, are dull, dull, dull.
2. It's easy to see in retrospect the campaigns where ads are done in a group or where a complete promotion package is put together at one time. Invariably the

quality is more uniform and higher. Even an integrated campaign done ad by ad tends to run downhill as agency and client people chip away at the edges.

3. Every advertising program we applauded somehow conveyed enthusiasm. It read like the person who produced it was interested and excited about the product, the company, or the sales proposition.

4. Some good sales ideas and some good writing was lost in overdesign or overproduction. Sometimes we forget that the purpose of advertising is to communicate, not simply to present a variety of shapes and colors in interesting or unusual combinations.

5. So it is with type. Type is for reading, not decorating.

6. The best advertising we did was fairly simple and proceeded step by step from an interesting start to a logical conclusion. Sometimes it was a long walk and sometimes a short walk, but with the good advertising the direction, the pace and the purpose are easy to trace.

September, 1970

TO: Everyone

FROM: Wm. A. Marsteller

SUBJECT: TV Commercials

My seatmate on a Chicago flight the other day was a Professor in the English department at the University of Wisconsin. This came out in a "What business are you in?" conversation over what TWA hopefully called dinner.

In turn I said I worked for an advertising agency, another claim perhaps not beyond challenge. Anyway, this quickly triggered an attack on television. Like most such attacks it lumped programming and commercials together

24

and was based on no real analysis of what television is or how it works.

A clue to his general misunderstanding was his praise of SESAME STREET. Most TV critics approve of SESAME STREET, never realizing until they study it that it is simply a series of commercials, constructed exactly like the advertising on television.

The facts are that the best television commercials are more imaginative, better done, warmer and clearer than most programming. Whenever 30 minutes of good commercials are shown to critical, non-advertising audiences their invariable reaction is that they somehow didn't realize how many were so good.

It is also a fact that very few writers or critics could begin to write an acceptable 30-second commercial. To put into five to eight frames and 50 to 60 words a complete story, is a far more demanding job than most writers ever face. I tried to get my seatmate to try in the time left before O'Hare, but he burrowed behind *Harper's*.

If, instead of philosophically attacking TV, advertising colleges ran a course in actually writing it, I think two things would happen:

1. The courses would be among the most popular on the campus.
2. There would be a lot better prose in the world.

Unfortunately many writers seem to feel there is a certain elegance in obfuscation, windiness and a casual sense of direction. One way to get over that quickly is to see if you're good enough and disciplined enough to write a 30-second commercial.

And then, try a 10-second ID.

November, 1970

TO: Everyone

FROM: Wm. A. Marsteller

SUBJECT: Unheard Sounds

About the only thing I recollect from second grade was one thing our otherwise unmemorable teacher told us.

She said that if a giant sequoia was struck by lightning and crashed to the ground there was no sound if no one was there to hear it. She said sound existed only if it was heard.

I think about that when I see a batch of PR feature stories. I used to write notes of praise if I thought they were well done. Now I first ask if any publication accepted them.

It's the same with advertising. Job applicants love to show you their "really best" work that somehow never got approved and never ran.

Professor Theodore Levitt of Harvard has written learnedly and interestingly on his thesis that there is no shortage of originality in business. The scarce commodity, he says, is the person who can conceive unique ideas and see them through to adoption.

If you are to do work of economic worth, then clearly it must be produced, printed or aired. To accomplish this requires an acute sensitivity to the audience, the sponsor, the product and the proposition, all of which can easily be submerged below an even more acute sensitivity to one's own ego.

Which is by no means to speak out for hack work or low standards. Precisely the opposite.

It is instead to honor those people of rare value who set high standards and are then driven to find the way to bring their creation to a broad and approving world of readers and listeners.

All others, however clever, make no sound.

Observations on People

Bill Marsteller's respect for, understanding for, and empathy with the people who work in his agency are quickly evident. Even when he makes empirical statements you have the feeling he doesn't quite take himself seriously. He can be sympathetic without becoming maudlin, and he has been able to be the chief executive without the appearance of a chief dictator. In these memos about people—their interests, their strengths and their weaknesses—his respect for the dignity of the individual shows through.

TO: Everyone

FROM: Wm. A. Marsteller

SUBJECT: People I Don't Understand

I don't understand people who never look out the window on a plane and who never use the map in the seat pocket.

I don't understand people who, in a strange city, want to be driven instead of renting a car and finding their own way.

Or people who can go to a supermarket and only buy the things they came for.

I don't understand people without a sense of loyalty or people who find disenchantment chic.

Or people who avoid talking to taxi drivers.

Or men who prefer men.

Or habitual cynics who are quick to criticize, slow to praise and add nothing of value.

I don't understand people who aren't upset if they miss an easy putt.

I don't understand closed-minded people who call themselves liberals.

I understand why some people are stuffy, but I don't understand how stuffy people can be oblivious to their own stuffiness.

I don't understand farm writers who hate the farm, or soap writers who think it quaint to do a wash, or valve

29

writers who can be satisfied without occasional visits to power plants or oil refineries.

Or speech writers who don't make speeches.

I don't understand dumb Kansans who won't listen to smart New Yorkers. Or dumb New Yorkers who sneer at smart Kansans.

I don't understand people who can live in Rome without bothering to learn Italian.

I don't understand people who are proud of their low threshold of ambition.

I don't understand people who, able to run, only walk slowly.

I don't understand people who listen only for dissonance and cacophony and sniff after that which is putrid.

Or those people who are sighted, but with so much to see and absorb, choose partial blindness as a way of life.

I don't understand those who find it so hard to say, "I love you."

And therefore, I don't understand those people who spend a lifetime in our business without discovering the elements of achievement and happiness.

October 25, 1962

TO: Everyone

FROM: Wm. A. Marsteller

SUBJECT: On the Pursuit of Security

Every child learns that the way to succeed in business (or the arts, professions, or, for that matter, crime) is by ability and hard work.

Then, somewhere along the line, he finds out there is another way—through what the English call "toadying," and we call "politics" or, depending upon the audience, something much less delicate.

But toadying, while historically looked down upon, is widely practiced in business today.

It is, almost invariably, a certain sign of incompetence, lack of self-confidence and maladjustment.

Company politics and apple polishing are usually more prevalent in administrative departments in large companies, where standards of individual performance are less exact and where corporate size is at least a temporary screen.

Even in our kind of business, though, toadying can be practiced for awhile, often with apparent success. The toady in our business tends to turn his attention to the client, rather than toward his own management, and with a happy client, he seems to have taken out job insurance. Toadying the client is not too difficult to spot, actually. It is usually characterized by excessive entertainment, by giving the client whatever he wants whether it is professionally sound or not, by talking big and writing small, by low account profitability, and, almost universally, by overpreoccupation with industry rumors and gossip.

With practice, you can spot the toady instinctively in any habitat, but if you want to become competent quickly in toady-spotting, you can take a cram course in one luncheon session in any mid-town New York restaurant that combines these characteristics: excessive prices, imposing decor and mediocre food. This is an irresistible combination to the totally addicted toady.

The toady weaves himself a cloak of intrigue, flattery, condescension, subjugation and gifts, and very often it comes out fine and fashionable and its wearer seems very grand indeed.

It is only when it is abruptly stripped away that the secret is out: the toady wears nothing underneath. There he stands, shivering and pathetic, a frightened man whose wardrobe was repossessed because he couldn't keep up the payments.

So it is with the account executive who tries to buy client satisfaction with food and drink. (Another account executive for another agency can always buy more.)

31

So it is with the advertising manager or public relations director who accepts truckling instead of truth and Christmas in place of creativity.

And so it is with agencies, too. At least two of our traditional rivals have had their cloaks flapping ominously of late.

But it is the individual toady we should pity.

One came to see me a week ago. After 15 years with a large corporation, he's been out of a job for six months. The man he guessed would be the next Sales VP didn't get the promotion and all those years of shining shoes now add up to just a lot of years of shining shoes. He's 42, with three kids in high school, and scared as hell. He has no self-confidence and it shows in a job interview. But you can't develop self-confidence sniveling.

A couple of weeks ago I watched another middle-aged man tremble in the corner while he waited to see how much of his conniving would be kicked out of the shadows for his management to see. What a way to live—a constant struggle to cover up ineptitude and a constant yearning for respect and recognition!

And in my mail is an application from an ex-Chicago agency man who wanted to come with us six or seven years ago with a pretty good account he controlled. We weren't interested in buying business, but even if we had been we'd have thought twice about it since the work he was doing for the client was pretty pedestrian. Someone was sure to tell the client someday it wasn't getting its money's worth, and somebody finally did. The agency in which our friend had landed shook itself once, and our friend fell off. Without an account and with no real ability he's been through four jobs since.

What started this piece was an article I read the other day about a survey among college students concerning the things they most wanted in a job. The article pointed out that after World War II studies showed that young people were much more security minded than they used to be.

"Security" was the No. 1 thing; compensation, achievement, promotion and such had become square. The article pointed out that the welfare state and the welfare company were accepted as a way of life. But in the last two years, similar surveys show a falling off in the popularity of security. A college placement officer was quoted as saying, "More of our young people feel that 'security' may be illusory and that competence may be the best hedge against the future."

And, of course, that's what security is all about.

June 4, 1969

TO: Everyone

FROM: Wm. A. Marsteller

SUBJECT: The Common Thread

Last week two things happened that prompted a little research that in turn prompts this memo.

The first was a mail questionnaire from a young advertising student in the Midwest starting to work on his Ph.D. His project is to determine what the key executives of major agencies have in common, and he was asking our observations.

The second was an interview with a 48-year-old man we have known slightly for 20 years, during which time he has worked for seven agencies in Chicago and New York in important management positions. He left his last job December 31, because he says he was "just plain bored," and now, five months later, for the first time in his career he can't find a job. Under "Accomplishments" at the end of his resume, he makes a virtue out of the fact that the chief executives of four of the top 25 agencies once reported to him.

But they are great successes and he can't get a job at

The Wonderful World of Words

anything like his top salary. Another of his problems is that he's never stayed anywhere long enough to build up an equity in fringe benefits.

What did these four men who used to work for him have that he didn't?

Not inheritance. None of them is in family-directed businesses.

Not education. All were college graduates, two from less well-known schools than his.

Not area of specialization. Two of the four worked for him in creative jobs and two in account handling.

But while our friend was working for seven agencies the other four are at the top of agencies they've worked for since their twenties.

Let's take a look at some of the big successes in the agency business and see what they have in common.

Norm Strouse, who retired recently as head of J. Walter Thompson, never went to college, and worked up through account handling and administrative jobs. He also never worked anywhere but JWT. Dan Seymour, his successor, made it through radio and TV, and, after ten years at Y & R, settled in at Thompson for 13 years of steady progress to the top.

Marion Harper, who left McCann-Erickson a rich man, started there as a trainee and worked nowhere else. He was a research man. Bob Healy, his successor, worked for Colgate for 18 years, then McCann for 16 years. Neal Gilliatt, next key man, started there in 1946, his first job.

Ed Bond, chief executive at Young & Rubicam, went to Kenyon & Eckhardt out of college, then into the service, and to Y & R in 1946 where he's been ever since, mostly in account work. Steve Frankfurt, President of Y & R, is a product of the creative department. It was his only agency. Our director, Joe Wilkerson, who retired as Executive Vice President of Y & R, worked in nearly every department, dating back to 1940. Y & R was his only agency.

Phil Schaff, Chairman of Leo Burnett, never worked anywhere else. Jock Elliott, head of Ogilvy, worked 15

34

years at BBD&O, then to O & M. Charlie Brower, Chairman, and Tom Dillon, President, of BBD&O, never worked anywhere else.

That's about all they have in common, in our opinion.

Chuck Winston and Dick Tully, who made it to the top at Foote, Cone & Belding, have been there since 1947 and 1946 respectively, right out of service. Archie Foster, an account man become President of Bates, has been there 14 years. Vic Bloede, a copywriter become President of Benton & Bowles, went there 19 years ago after three years in one other agency. Paul Harper and Jim Isham, top men at Needham, Harper & Steers, have been on hand for over 20 years in both creative and account work. Carl Nichols and Tony Chevins, top men at Cunningham & Walsh and both out of creative, have been there almost their entire time in the business.

Cy Schneider, President of Carson/Roberts, started there as a trainee. So did Ed Parrack at Ketchum, MacLeod & Grove. Joe Daly, Doyle Dane Bernbach President, tried one other agency for three years, then went to DDB in 1949. Tom Adams and Ernie Jones, heads of Campbell-Ewald and MacManus, John & Adams, started with their agencies as trainees. Herb Strauss, head of Grey, has been there since 1939.

Public relations is a newer business, but in the older firms, the pattern is the same. At Hill & Knowlton, Bert Goss came aboard in 1944 after twelve years of teaching and newspapering, and Dick Darrow, after ten years as an editor and PR director, joined H & K in 1952.

George Hammond has had virtually his entire career at Carl Byoir, and Bob Wood, after four years of newspapering, joined the firm in 1946.

It works with us, too. Dick Christian and Buck Buchwald have never worked in another agency.

Obviously, just hanging around won't do it. It goes without saying that intelligence, ability, hard work, and accomplishment are requirements.

But it is equally clear, on the record, that the people

who stay put have far the best chance to get their achievements recognized in the most tangible of all ways.

June 13, 1969

TO: Everyone

FROM: Wm. A. Marsteller

SUBJECT: 21 Things I Have Learned in This Business

1. Dull people always write dull copy, but bright people only write bright copy when they work hard at it.
2. Many things contribute to a successful advertisement but the most important single element is an unmistakable identification of the product or the sponsor company.
3. Most successful PR placements are the result of finding a reader or listener or viewer need or interest and then fulfilling it. It is exactly the same with successful advertising.
4. The best way to improve your writing is to write. Every day. Including Christmas, Yom Kippur and the Fourth of July.
5. Every good creative person I ever met had a wide streak of self-doubt and self-criticism.
6. Client sales management can't resist a really good selling or merchandising idea, even if the budget is already spent. Yet they can sometimes resist a solid advertising idea, even if there is still money in the budget.
7. You can make a good PR man into a good advertising man (and vice versa) easier than you can make a mediocre PR man into a good PR man, or a mediocre advertising man into a good advertising man.
8. An ad is no good, no matter how well designed, if people don't come away with a strong idea.
9. If someone says of something you wrote, "I don't un-

derstand it," don't try to explain it. Just rewrite it so it's not only clear to you, but clear to him, too.

10. Every good boss I ever worked for gave me responsibility.

11. I am very nervous about the self-impressed hotshots who think they can wing it at a presentation. Even Laurence Olivier is better if he rehearses. Also me. Also you.

12. Most secretaries are more competent than their bosses take the trouble to discover.

13. No great orchestra was ever built by a man who continued his career as a soloist. Likewise for agencies.

14. From sending out and receiving hundreds of reference letters, as well as phone calls, I've come to two firm conclusions: (a) most people fib a little to a new employer about what they made on the job they are leaving; (b) most people fib a little to their friends at their old job about what they're getting at the new one.

15. If, like you, I find it hard to get the time to just sit back and think, I send out for a sandwich, shut the door, and have lunch at my desk.

16. There is no difference between men and women in the qualities that make good account executives or writers. Which is not to decry the difference between men and women.

17. Some people think visually and some people think verbally and some people don't think much at all. I see no advantage between the first two types.

18. Maintaining a neat desk and office creates less pressure than working under messy conditions. I used to work in a newspaper office and in a manufacturing plant; I've tried it both ways.

19. New Yorkers generally know a lot about sociology and very little about geography.

20. Two ads can look pretty much the same and still have an enormous difference in readership. Our house ads tell us this conclusively. So what our ad says must be very important.

37

21. Fish is better on the East Coast, salads are better on the West Coast, and steak and corn on the cob are best in the Midwest. Turnips are the same everywhere.

July 15, 1970

TO: Everyone

FROM: Wm. A. Marsteller

SUBJECT: Some Things I Know For Sure

Fifty per cent of advertising copywriters are descended from parrots, 35 per cent are descended from speechless peacocks, and the rest are descended straight from God.

If you cross out all the clichés in a new product release, you often get a fairly interesting story.

Three-day weekends are overrated.

Good account executives are very careful about detail, even though it bores them.

You can't administer successful employee relations programs for Midland, Texas, from New York City.

In general, American WASP cooking is very bad, as is Irish cooking. This explains Philadelphia.

There is no essential creative difference between consumer and industrial advertising, except that it's easier to write bad television than bad technical advertising.

To find out about a company or a product, two days making calls with a good salesman is worth two months of briefing by management.

New business presentations are like the racing form. Most of the necessary information is there, but hunch and emotion still color most bets. Then too, you never know when the fix is in.

Young people should eat lots of chocolate cake because they'll miss it so much when they get older.

There is a correlation between how much Walter Mitty you have in you and how creative you are.

People with a lot of ideas but not much ability at follow-through can get a company into a lot of trouble.

Arrogance is the antithesis of real communication.

March 15, 1972

TO: Everyone

FROM: Wm. A. Marsteller

SUBJECT: People I Can Do Without Very Nicely

1. People who delegate trivia but never delegate responsibility.
2. Office politicians.
3. People who take five ads to the art department at 4:50 P.M. Friday, on their way home, and expect finished layouts at 9:00 A.M. Monday. If they're in on time.
4. People who don't answer a ringing phone unless its theirs.
5. People who suck lemons in front of piccolo players.
6. People who think the client's business is a bore.
7. Girls who never dress like girls.
8. People who go around putting the knock on their own company but haven't the courage to quit.
9. People who don't treat secretaries as equals.
10. Secretaries who think they're doing us a favor to come to work.
11. People who are condescending to clients. Or to service departments.
12. People who push media reps or suppliers around.
13. Big Shots who are too important to learn our basic systems and procedures.
14. People who never pass the salt unless they're asked.

15. People who can't keep a confidence.
16. PR types who think they've outgrown writing anything themselves.
17. People with dirty fingernails.
18. People who call conferences and leave the conference room a mess afterward.
19. Writers who resist editing.
20. Girls who reek of Estee Lauder.
21. College students who send 25-page questionnaires expecting me to write their dumb thesis.
22. People who let their dogs lick you.
23. People like me who never listen.
24. All people who are self-important, self-centered and insensitive to others.

February 20, 1962

TO: Everyone

FROM: Wm. A. Marsteller

SUBJECT: An Anthology of Little Stories with Big Implications

Who Killed Creativity?

A few weeks ago a major food manufacturer in the Midwest abruptly changed agencies, despite the fact that the advertising the old agency had been preparing for nearly 20 years was highly creative, a frequent award winner, and the company's sales were quite healthy.

An impetuous decision?

I'm sure not.

A year ago I was in the manufacturer's city for a speech and was driven to the airport by the top account man in the old agency. As we were leaving the meeting, the Sales Vice President of the advertiser stopped us to remind the account

40

man that it was the 21st of the month and he hadn't gotten the monthly billing yet.

"Look," he said. "Don't you guys realize we can't run our business that way, even if you can. For God's sake get your accounting department up to date; if we have billing spilling over into the next budget year again, somebody's head is going to roll, and I promise you it won't be mine!"

It wasn't.

Home is Where You're Happy

Next one, courtesy of a secretary in our NY office, who used to work for an agency which shall go nameless.

She still has friends there and had lunch with some of the girls the other day. Here's her report:

"A big advertiser is changing agencies and, before asking any of them to make a presentation, is visiting them first.

"This agency is in a pretty old building and is kind of a mess generally. The advertiser visitors looked around and went on their way. The agency wasn't invited into the finals and the advertiser made no bones about why not.

" 'We just wouldn't feel comfortable about having our account in your shop. We run an orderly business and we think we need an orderly agency.' "

Eager Beaver, Southern Style

Ever hear about how Harold Burson became a part of this Company?

We were very new and Rockwell was nearly 40 per cent of our business. Rockwell ordered a helicopter for executive travel and felt it deserved heavy publicity treatment. We had no New York facilities for follow-through on this assignment, so I came to New York and called on five or six editors.

"What small publicity firm in New York do you most

41

respect?" I asked, after outlining the problem and the opportunity. I got a dozen names but two were on nearly every list. Harold Burson Public Relations was one of the two, and I wrote Harold and also the principal of the other company.

In two days I had a detailed air mail reply from Harold. The following day, he was in my office in Chicago. Within a week after he got our letter he was earning his fee on his new client.

Two weeks later I got a reply from the other firm, well-written, completely documented, just as good as Harold's, only not nearly so soon.

The other firm hasn't been in the telephone book in years.

On the Building of an Image

Next, the last paragraph of a report from Art Cowles in Pittsburgh to Dick Christian, reporting on a meeting last week of the ABP Awards Jury, of which Art was a member:

"To warm the cockles of Mr. Marsteller's heart, your friend and mine, Ralph Winslow, Chairman of the Judges (and Advertising VP of Koppers Co.), gave public utterance to the fact that all of the non-agency judges showed up on time, but that only one agency head was there on time. If there were any doubts as to who the agency head was, I would not mention it here. Of such things are images built."

An Element of Pricing

Now from my files, a two-year-old letter from the president of a large Chicago engraving company:

"As I told you yesterday, we have raised our base for all customers but you. Of course, one reason is that we get such a large volume of business from you without any commissions to a salesman.

"But I think you ought to know that we handle your work with less overhead than any customer we have because your production department and art department

are so careful about details. When work comes from you, it is ready for the camera, clearly marked and clean.

"We like working with Fred, Ed, Jack and Paul, and everyone else in your shop, and I think you ought to know it."

October 12, 1965

TO: Everyone

FROM: Wm. A. Marsteller

SUBJECT: Turnover

Although industry generally keeps careful figures on employee turnover, no standard statistics are available for the advertising and public relations fields, where turnover presumably is high.

Recently an advertising association made a pilot study to see if it could get cooperation in developing turnover statistics, and if this study is to be trusted, our turnover rate is about half the average.

Turnover in our kind of a business is difficult to assess. In many agencies it is the direct result of group layoffs following lost business. This kind of turnover we have very little of, partly because we haven't had much account turnover.

On the other hand, undeniably we do have a higher turnover than most of our clients, and sometimes this is hard for them to understand. There are a good many reasons for our higher rate.

The first one is that there are simply no adequate pre-employment tests that even approximate accuracy in identifying the peculiar blend of creativity and motivation and sound business sense that are the principal ingredients of success in our business. So we still rely more than we would like to on trial-and-error methods of identifying good peo-

43

ple. Probably the biggest contributor to our personnel turnover is the correction of our hiring mistakes.

The second reason for high turnover is that we are constantly pushing our performance standards upward. Stories that might have been released by Burson-Marsteller ten years ago, ads that went out for client approval ten years ago, don't get past the creative screening and editing processes today. As standards go up, fewer people can meet them, and some leave from the realization that they might find success easier elsewhere. Or at least they may find it easier to avoid exposure.

The third reason is that we are growing some able, rounded people who are attractive to others, and especially clients. We have just lost a senior man to a client who came to recognize in him talents and broad abilities not in oversupply in his own organization. I know of at least three people who, within the last two months, have turned down flattering offers from clients, but the offers were there. One of the penalties of seeking out the best people we can find, and then exposing them to responsibility, training and the discipline of high standards is that we are going to be shot at by the head-hunters. GE knows this well. So we'll lose some good people, but we'll keep a lot, too.

Finally, some of the turnover comes from the nature of the people who gravitate to this business. Good advertising and public relations people look for new challenges, new assignments, new outlets for their creative abilities. Unfortunately clients are reluctant to let us rotate people as much as we would like. They tend to overestimate the value of detailed product and market knowledge (which they possess themselves) and to underestimate the value of fresh, uninhibited promotional ideas. We are working harder at this problem, as you will recognize from some of the account shifts this year, but solutions come slowly.

Scuttlebutt tells you other reasons for turnover, but as human nature tells you, the man or woman who doesn't make it here is most likely to blame us, or working conditions, or The System. It takes a self-confident and honest

person to administer self-blame, and that kind of person changes jobs the very least.

Certainly we want to emphasize employment stability rather than turnover, but as in most things, what we seek is moderation, rather than total abstinence. If we don't correct our bad guesses in hiring, if we don't bring about creative self-renewal, if we don't go after the best people because we are afraid someone will steal them from us, then our product will soon be as dry and decaying as that other monument to total abstinence, the W.C.T.U.

November 22, 1961

TO: Everyone

FROM: Wm. A. Marsteller

SUBJECT: Rod Reed

I first met Rod Reed in 1945.

I was prepared not to like him.

He was manager of The McCarty Company's Pittsburgh office, the advertising agency which was handling what is now the Rockwell Manufacturing Company. He came out to East Chicago to see me at Edward Valves to review our advertising programs since we had just become part of Rockwell, through a merger.

I didn't want anybody telling me anything about my advertising.

But things didn't work out the way I expected. Rod's attitude, from the minute he sat down at my desk, was "What have you learned that will help us with *all* of Rockwell's advertising?"

Within five minutes, he was my friend.

Later, he became a friend of a good many of you . . . all of you, I think, who really knew him.

But some of you are new, and never had a chance to

know about Rod—to know the kind of a person he was, or to know how much of an imprint he made on this Company. Rod hated public speaking, but he was a wonderful companion, and, man-to-man, he had immense personal charm. He laughed easily, he listened well, and he told fascinating, self-deprecating stories.

I loved to hear him talk about his experiences when, as a young civil engineering graduate of Brown, he laid out the roads in Sing Sing prison. Or to hear him describe his job as advertising manager of Pittsburgh Equitable Meter, which he said—in order of importance—involved seeing that the rest-rooms were clean, the mail distributed early, the suggestion box emptied of gum wrappers, that the storeroom didn't run out of paper clips, and that an ad was prepared for convention issues of a few magazines.

Later, I was Rod's client, and no happier agency-client relationship ever existed. Rod worked very hard to make it so. I remember once, when orders had come to me that we had to have a certain ad in the next issue of a certain magazine, I passed those orders on to Rod who said it couldn't be done, and I said it better be. It was, but I didn't know until weeks later that to be sure there was no final slip, Rod had taken a plane from Pittsburgh to Albany to personally deliver the plate to the printer.

Rod and I became partners almost accidentally. I had resigned from Rockwell to start a marketing counsel business in Chicago. In December, 1950, my last month at Rockwell, I went to a holiday cocktail party at Al Rockwell's house. L. A. Dixon, Rockwell's executive vice president, was talking with Rod and me at the party. He casually said that we ought to team up—that it was becoming increasingly difficult to handle Rockwell advertising through several agencies and particularly he wanted to coordinate the Delta advertising in Milwaukee and the Nordstrom advertising, then handled on the Coast, into a single organization.

Next day, Rod and I talked with Geb Gebhardt, who ran a small agency in Chicago and was a friend of both of ours,

and within a week we had bought T. T. McCarty's interest in the Pittsburgh McCarty operation and merged it with Geb's Chicago operation to form Marsteller, Gebhardt and Reed. Rod continued to head the Pittsburgh operation.

Rod loved being an account executive but hated being a general manager. As far as I know, he never fired anyone. He had no trouble praising good work, but it was punishment to him if he had to be critical. He suffered physically if circumstances forced him to hurt someone's feelings. But he liked making ads, and he made a lot of them—good ones. In ten years, on accounts he handled, I doubt if we have had more than a couple of extensions a year.

In the last couple of years, Rod had a series of health problems, and when finally he was able to shed some of the responsibilities of day-to-day management of the Pittsburgh office, he said it was as if a big load had been taken off his shoulders. But nothing ever kept him from handling his accounts with distinction and dedication.

As a senior officer of the Company, as one of our major stockholders, and as a director, he always put the good of the Company first. It was typical that it was he who proposed to the Board of Directors that our name be shortened. This had been proposed by a variety of people outside and inside the Company for a long time. I never felt it was necessary or even desirable, but the majority did, and Rod resolved the matter for them.

When the words "Reed" and "Gebhardt" went out of our firm name, I felt we were giving up something that was a part of my life, a part of my own business career. I was never flattered by the proposal, and I wish now I had never permitted it.

And now, not only are their names gone, but in less than a year, both Rod and Geb are gone.

This I must say to you all:

This Company will always have some of Rod and some of Geb in it. And all of us are the better for it.

47

Policies, Practices and Operations

Successful performance of any business, in Bill Marsteller's view, depends on sound policies clearly enunciated, on efficient practices in getting the work done, and on daily operations in which people at all levels can take satisfaction in contributing their diverse talents to a common effort.

The following memoranda sample his communications on these subjects.

TO: All Male Personnel

FROM: Emily Post Marsteller

SUBJECT: The Day That Marilyn Dropped In

A soft, insinuating, love-laden voice said, "Am I intruding?"

I looked up from my desk, and nearly slid on to the floor. Standing there, more lovely than in any picture, was America's sex goddess, Marilyn Monroe.

Her soft blonde hair, hanging loosely to her shoulders, shimmered in the sun. Her eyes were deep and clear and somehow sympathetic and understanding. Her full red lips were parted just slightly, almost as if inside, she was panting with excitement. Her yellow-gold knit dress was form-tight, clearly outlining her high, firm bosom, her flat stomach, her exquisitely rounded hips, and her splendidly symmetrical thighs.

I recovered, only enough to ask, "Won't you sit down?"

She crossed her legs, and then I noticed.

Instead of stockings, she was wearing ankle socks that came up only two inches above her shoes. Above them, her legs were covered with a thick, matted growth of black hair.

I threw up in the waste basket.

* * *

Now fellas, if Marilyn Monroe can't get away with it, how come you think you can?

51

And shaving your legs won't help much either. Even those of you who ain't so hairy, tend to have awfully white legs, often with goose bumps.

Very few companies have more people with good looking legs than this company, in my opinion, but they are all on the girls.

I have the feeling that our clients aren't knocked out with our legs either.

Perhaps I'm getting old, but I'm getting more conscious of men's legs between the tops of these silly little ankle socks and the high rise of trousers when seated. It's sloppy and unbusinesslike. You don't need to wear garters to avoid it. At all price ranges there are now socks on the market at various lengths that stay up without garters, even on skinny legs. I know.

For golf, tennis, sailing or a 25 yard dash around the bedroom, that's your business.

Are you still with me?

If so, let's go on to the next problem.

Sport jackets.

When we open our office in Waterloo, Ia., all the staff ought to wear them every day. Everybody in Waterloo does. When in Waterloo, do as the Waterloons.

But take New York or Chicago, for instance, as we are trying very hard to do.

If you are an artist or a production manager, you suffer enough already, so if you're in the office all day, O.K. But, generally, if you are going to be out, calling on clients, or you are going to have outsiders calling on you, wear a suit, huh?

You can tell me some of our clients wear sport jackets to work.

All I know is I never saw the head of a single client company in a big city in a sport jacket in the office.

I would also add that they mostly have clean finger nails, but I never saw them work on them in my presence.

52

As far as I know, they have clean noses, but I don't recall any of them picking them in a conference.

And I expect they itch as much as I do sometimes, but if they scratch in public, they're pretty sneaky about it.

You still here?

O.K., then about smoking.

I smoke. I like to smoke. I don't intend to quit.

But some people don't like smoking in their office. And some people don't like cigars or pipes at all.

So I never, never light up in a stranger's office unless and until he does. And I never smoke a pipe or cigar unless there is evidence he does.

I know you wouldn't do that either, so I probably shouldn't even bring it up.

Never, never, never smoke during a presentation, inside or out. No smokes on the podium.

Now:

Do I do something I ought to know about?

Write me.

Anonymously, of course.

May 4, 1971

MEMO: To Everyone

FROM: W. A. Marsteller

SUBJECT: Do Clothes Make the Man?

Of course not, although it is widely believed they sometimes make the woman. They don't even successfully disguise the man for long.

You can dress eccentric as hell, but if you can only write or draw or think eccentric, your commercial value will soon be established as negative.

53

I keep interviewing alleged creative people, and I'll tell you that a lot of these wild rags are just a security blanket. A good creative person doesn't have to look like he or she or it was conceived in the exhaust pipe of a motorcycle.

On the other hand, if you've got it and a reasonable number of people in addition to you think so, you can flaunt it and dress like you just blew the Manson ranch and still make out nice.

Up to a point. If your ambition is to get a lot of your things approved at the client, you've either got to leave that to the comb and brush crowd or strike some bourgeois compromise yourself. You know, sell out to the system like Bill Bernbach or Mary Wells.

None of which is to say that a white shirt and a crew cut is any better disguise if down deep you're shallow. A blue serge suit doesn't beget dependability. There are a lot of recorded cases where vice presidents who dressed like Herbert Hoover took off with Myrtle, the teller in cage No. 3, along with a duffel bag packed with a lavender and pink sport shirt and $206,431 worth of stuff he was watching for widows and orphans.

There may be some kind of satisfaction in being 'way ahead of or 'way behind the norm of the place and time. But those satisfactions are mickey mouse compared to the satisfactions of moving things, of moving people, of getting things printed or spieled.

There is, as the liquor people always tell you correctly if not always convincingly, a happy medium.

Just remember, the freak show is never in the main tent.

December 23, 1965

TO: Everyone

FROM: Wm. A. Marsteller

SUBJECT: Ho Ho Ho

One of your associates who formerly labored at one of the Madison Avenue communications Dachaus points out that we are not upholding tradition. We do not engage in the Rites of the Season, and he misses them.

For example, as he says, we do not have Christmas bashes.

When we were very new we had a couple with sorry results. A building employee got zonked on our premises using our prune juice and then walked into an automobile as he left the building. In another of our locations a secretary took dead aim on a Member of Management, who no doubt had it coming but felt compelled to Restructure the Office after Jan. 1. Then there was the case of the Irate Husband who got me out of bed, long distance, at 3:00 A.M. Xmas morning to tell me that his bride had not yet returned from our office party.

Things like that leave scars. Therefore, no more Company-sponsored bacchanalia.

It also seems to be seasonal in the communications dodge to have a Message From the Master.

Each year a prominent agency head rents a hall, hangs up some holly, and lectures his little ones on the kind of employees he likes and the kind he doesn't like. This cheers everybody up immensely.

McGraw-Hill sends its general staff on the road to hold little meetings with the outlying offices. This permits outlying people to talk, face to face, to the Very Top Management and vice versa. Neither team seems very comfortable about it. Also, since there are so many offices and what with

one thing and another, the confrontations often drag on into mid-January, a time when most people are naturally surly.

This same policy is followed by several of the largest agencies. The president of one has confided that he has never been in Chicago when it wasn't snowing or Los Angeles when it wasn't raining, which gives you some idea about Good Will Toward Men.

Several agency heads use this time of year to make grudging reports to their Fellow Employees on the condition of Your Company. These reports are often beautifully gift wrapped, but when you open them up somebody forgot to put in the present. There is, for instance, the well-known mid-Western agency which annually calls the troops in from the rice paddies to explain why victory has eluded them for one more year and that there will therefore be no profit sharing.

We don't even have the Inexpensive, Funny Gift Exchange. We tried that once, too. You know, you draw a name and you give them a present ("Be sure not to spend more than $2.00, and make it FUNNY!") and you never know who drew your name, only there's always a couple of finks who tell. We went through this, too. One girl started bawling in front of everyone when, instead of an invitation to stop for a drink with an art director, she got a tube of Clearasil.

Of course some of these yuletide traditions are not denied you; they are merely vested upon you at other times of the year. Often continuously. For instance, the Message from the Master.

Also, the chicken colonels in this outfit are moving around the country constantly, being friendly, mixing up names, making uninformed comments on your work, and things like that. It isn't seasonal.

And it's true we do bring our Fellow Associates together once a year for financial disclosure and mutual admiration. The way we're different is we do it in late January, when, as we have pointed out, people are in their most quarrel-

some mood and least likely to be taken in by half facts. So we open the books much wider than most of our non-public competitors and you can look without fear of getting your nose pinched when the ledgers are slammed shut after one peek.

All of this is not to imply that Your Management is anti-tradition or anti-Christmas, although some of them are type-cast for Dickens.

It's just that we think that your religion, your children, your family, and your own traditions are very personal things.

We cannot interpret the holiday season for you, and it is meddlesome and demeaning to try.

We shouldn't intrude into your observance or nonobservance with business irrelevancies. We even had some misgivings about organizing the gifts for the children of Marsteller, Pa., but the outpouring of generosity from all our offices apparently sets this apart.

That's about all, except one announcement.

Since we distributed cranberries at Thanksgiving, there will be no mailing of pistachio nuts for Christmas.

Have a Happy Holiday anyway.

Each in your own way.

September 23, 1964

TO: Everyone

FROM: Wm. A. Marsteller

SUBJECT: COMMUNICATIONS I—Freedom of Speech

Word reaches me that at the last meeting of our Operating Committee there was quite a rhubarb about whether or not one of our employees should make speeches or write articles taking a position contrary to the expressed view of the Company management.

Our leaders got caught up on the whole problem of freedom of speech that has troubled so many for so long. The principles seem so clear, but the application of the principles can be so clouded.

For instance, take the recent academic freedom cases that got the University of Illinois much unwanted publicity.

First, an associate professor wrote a letter to a newspaper advocating free love for one and all in the University community and he got the sack. Then another professor came along with a series of articles in praise of the John Birch Society, of which he was an officer, and he got not so much as a reprimand. The feeling was that, in the first case, the man's exercise of his individual rights impinged upon the rights of others, while, in the second case, the rights of others were not affected.

The love bug wrote his letter to the student newspaper. He signed it with his affiliation with the University of Illinois clearly indicated. It was timed to hit on the weekend of the state high school basketball tournament, when a maximum number of high school students and teachers, state legislators, clergymen and small town business leaders were in the audience. His letter was reprinted in all kinds of news media, and within a week highly-placed state legislators were making it clearly known that they had no intention of approving increases in faculty salaries, funds for new buildings, etc., and in fact were in favor of a rousing investigation of the South Campus after dark. It was also alleged that his class lectures had touched upon his interpretation of student morals.

So the University administration concluded that in the exercise of his own freedom the prof had gone a long way toward fouling things up for others. Out he went, to sue, as he is yet doing.

Comes now the prof who tilts right. He joined the John Birch Society as an individual. He made no attempt to inject his views into his teaching (his subject is non-politcal). He made no effort to distribute his writings to student, or

even local, media. No one threatened to cut off state funds to the University, although a few of the first prof's friends suggested an investigation. So he's still teaching.

A couple of years ago we had a similar problem in our Company. One of our people was hot for the Birch bit, too. He went around making speeches. So far, so good—his business, his right.

However, he had a mimeographed biographical sketch prepared which detailed his association with us rather clearly. After his lectures began turning up in newspapers with headlines that identified him as an officer or executive in our Company, clients began calling and asking unpleasant questions. There began to be evidence that we were about to lose a client or two because of our unhappy evangelist. Now, if someone else loses a job because we lose business, if your profit sharing is reduced because we lose business, how far can we go in protecting his right of freedom of speech?

In this case, he got so involved in his crusading that he forgot to do his job, so we dispensed with his services on the simple grounds of non-performance of duty.

What the Operating Committee was arguing about was nothing so deep as political freedom. It is a less elevated, but no less complex problem.

You start with the fact that we encourage our people to write articles and make speeches of a professional nature to express our leadership in a tangible and cumulative manner.

Then we act like we don't trust anyone, or we want to practice thought control, by saying we'd like management clearance of such articles and speeches.

There is, of course, a reason, and I hope it justifies the policy.

If one of our Vice Presidents writes an article for the trade press, signing it by his title and company, in which he advocates that ad managers be abolished and agencies deal directly with sales managers, he may be expressing a

59

deeply held view but it is one which will inevitably get you and me in trouble. We will be asked to comment, as a company. Do we agree? If not, what action will we take? Then perhaps the ad manager of one of the accounts on which the man works announces he is taking his account elsewhere. Our VP is certainly not the only one affected. There are art, production, media, his secretary, etc.

Suppose the facts are all the same except that he does not sign with his title and company? Does this change things?

Somewhat. As an officer of the company he is presumed, legally, to be speaking for the company when he identifies his rank and company.

On the other hand, quite clearly I could write such an article and only sign my name, and you'd be stuck with the consequences. I couldn't really divorce myself from the company in the public mind. Neither could Harold Burson or Dick Christian, and thereafter it becomes difficult to tell at what point an employee is more clearly identified as an individual than as a corporate spokesman.

The Burnett agency had this problem recently. A highly placed creative director wrote a book which painted advertising agencies as collections of unhappy people wasting away their lives in the promotion of products they regarded poorly.

Leo Burnett rushed to print to defend the right of the man to think and write such thoughts and then added that, of course, the man was inaccurate, and probably incompetent to observe. It is hard to see how the man can continue to have much value at Burnett. As a client, would you want this man who confesses acute nausea when writing about your product? As a fellow employee, would you want this guy next door with his finger pointed at you, calling out "Miserable Fourflusher"?

There are no pat answers, no clear policy, to cover all gradations of freedom of speech. You have to examine individual circumstances.

In any event, we respect and defend your right to think and write and speak as you please, remembering always

that rights are not unilateral, and that there is an always present possibility that the excessive exercise of your own rights may ruin the rights of others.

September 30, 1964

TO: Everyone

FROM: Wm. A. Marsteller

SUBJECT: COMMUNICATIONS II—Tell All

Sometime during the 1930's, during a period when Franklin D. Roosevelt used businessmen for logs for his fireside chats, the "tell all" theory of employee communications was born.

During this time, when business was widely pictured as a vast conspiracy to subjugate the American working class, businessmen began programs to inform their employees of all kinds of inner workings of their companies. Unfortunately, most employees were improperly prepared to deal with all this information. A statement that Company X was seeking a new bank loan was assumed to be an indication of coming bankruptcy. An announcement that a company was going to build a plant addition caused consternation because employees, far from interpreting it as a positive move, saw it as a prelude to new technologies with which they were unfamiliar and preferred to so remain.

Anyway, after 15 years or so, *Fortune* ran a series on the perils of corporate overcommunication.

Some of our management has been recently troubled by this old communications problem. What should you tell the troops about what the management is up to?

For instance.

We recently dismissed an account executive. We made no public announcement of this always unpleasant action, not wanting to hurt the man and not being particularly

61

proud of guessing wrong in hiring him. He, however, did not go quietly. He made the rounds of a number of offices telling his associates how poorly he had been treated, how little notice he had been given, how we were on the verge of losing at least one of the accounts upon which he had toiled, and how he had been given absolutely no reason for the discharge, and how, some Friday, it will happen to you.

At the Management meeting in June there was long discussion of how we should perhaps send out notices to folks around the house when something like this happens so that people can judge the facts more fairly.

Therefore, I have prepared a prototype release for the next such case, with the facts based on the last one.

"Effective at 5:00 o'clock Friday, John Jones is being fired as Account Executive in our New York office.

"He was hired seven months ago after being interviewed by three men. Two of the three had doubts at the time but he showed such good samples and his last boss praised him so highly that we decided to take a chance.

"Unfortunately, it developed that his samples were done by others and his reference was good largely because his last company was anxious to avoid a long unemployment insurance claim.

"It developed he simply could not meet our standards, as to either quality or quantity. Further, one of our clients reported that the man had made disparaging remarks about both his supervisor and our Company. We found this not difficult to believe since he constantly made disparaging remarks about the client to us.

"He has had two employee evaluations and has been told in short, simple words that his work was unsatisfactory. He has read his own employee evaluation, and thanked his supervisor for being so frank and helpful. However, his attitude will likely be quite different on Friday afternoon.

"To minimize account handling difficulties we have told

the clients on whose accounts he has been working that he is to be replaced. One said: 'I don't recall him.' The other said: 'Thank God!'

"Naturally we wish him well and want to do everything we can to help him get another job."

January 14, 1966

TO: Everyone

FROM: Wm. A. Marsteller

SUBJECT: The Profit Motive

Spies among you tell me that from time to time our hallowed halls have heard whispers that we are profit oriented.

A few of the more brazen have even spoken directly about this matter to members of the overhead stratum.

There seems to be a concern that we sometimes put profitability ahead of creativity. This is fuzzy-wuzzy thinking. Profitability doesn't beget creativity; creativity seems to beget profitability.

There are some illustrations in the public domain.

Doyle, Dane, Bernbach, every man's choice as a creative house, is also disclosed to be among the very most profitable. Ted Bates, which has one of the five living members of the copywriters' Hall of Fame, has been pursued by Mr. Whiskers for a redistribution of its not inconsiderable retained earnings. Carson/Roberts, generally believed to be (next to us, of course) the most creative shop on the West Coast, is also generally believed to be among the most profitable and affluent.

And, if you want, you can find little clues around our own nest.

Looking over the individual account profitability records for the past year, with one or two exceptions the accounts

63

that are the most solidly profitable are the same darn ones we keep using in new business presentations to illustrate our creative skills.

So I get a little bored when I still hear that we sacrifice creativity on the pyre of profits. It just ain't so. The facts read the other way.

Why do people think so?

I wish I really knew.

Sometimes I think it is simply the desire, conscious or unconscious, to place the blame elsewhere when we realize we have produced an undistinguished piece of work. It is easier to say, "I need more help," or "I don't have time to think," or "All they think of is billing," than it is to judge one's own work harshly.

But maybe it isn't that at all. Maybe it's just the foolish legend that creative people are improvident, that creativity and prosperity do not live in the same house.

Yet this isn't so, as you can quickly establish for yourself by ticking off the authors of the most creative things you have read, seen and heard.

Let us lay this creative vs. profit confusion to rest. We can, we should and we will have the best of both.

However, if you don't agree—if you really feel that our creativity suffers because of our solvency—there is a way to express your view:

You can burn your profit sharing certificate.

April 25, 1963

TO: Everyone

FROM: Wm. A. Marsteller

SUBJECT: How to Get Promoted

Last Saturday I was cleaning out some files (you could, too, you know) and I came across a memo I had written

64

five or six years ago to one of our Bright Young Men who wanted to know how to get promoted.

I showed the memo to Dick Christian and he thought you might be interested in it.

Here are the suggestions I made:

1. If you want to be a business manager, think like a business manager. Ask yourself what your reaction would be if you were running the business and someone else was doing what you are about to do. Respect the necessity of chain of command even when you don't respect every link in the chain.
2. Be loyal. Don't just be loyal to me or to the Company as a name, but to the people who make up the Company.
3. Reserve your opinions of people, good or bad, until you've observed them and lived with them long enough to be sure you're right.
4. Quit worrying about your competition. The only real competitor you will ever have is yourself. Remember, I don't pick our leaders; the followers do.
5. Look for the best in others and remember all of us have more weaknesses than we see in ourselves.
6. Be interested in the other man's job. Make suggestions humbly. Ask advice. Build up your associates —to each other, to media representatives and editors, to friends, neighbors, your family and visitors from our other offices.
7. In your dealings with production, art, media, accounting and all service departments—ask, don't order.
8. Do your job well whether anyone else does his well or not.
9. Don't waste your abilities—write articles, make speeches. Stand out from the crowd or be lost in the crowd.
10. Keep trying to improve the work you ask your clients to approve. And remember, no matter how

right you are they'll only accept your suggestions gradually, usually only in part, and not at all unless they both respect you and like you.

11. If you have problems, doubts or suggestions about the management of this business, go to the management with your comments, not to the guy at the next desk. He can't do anything about it.

12. Remember that you are sometimes wrong and so am I. I have often been on the losing side of a vote at the Board of Directors' meeting. I accept the judgment of the majority.

13. Never quit creating. The world is run by creative people.

14. Remember that most of your clients and some of your associates are not as quick as you are when it comes to communications techniques. Patience is hard but rewarding.

15. Stay out of cliques. You will need everyone's help and friendship if you are a boss, even if you could get to be one without it.

16. Other people like a compliment as much as you do.

17. Don't get discouraged. Look back at your progress, account by account, job by job, person by person. Thousands of good novels were never written because the author got bored or discouraged after the first chapter.

18. Enjoy your opportunities and take your frustrations as challenges. They'll balance out.

19. Put a "Pride" file in your desk. This is a file of the jobs you have done that you're really, really proud of. See how fast you can make it grow. Review it from time to time to see if the oldest entries now look ordinary to you. Great men grow.

20. Try not to worry about your title. The title you want most is one you'll never see typed on a letter. It's the title of "A Great Advertising Man." It is obtained through democratic election by common consent.

21. Never lose your sense of humor.
22. Don't take yourself too seriously.
23. Hang on to your humility.
24. Take your triumphs home to your wife and tell your troubles to the bartender or keep them to yourself.
25. Remember, almost no one holds a confidence. It's human nature to pass along stories. Be sure when you tell tales about someone else that you're willing to have the subject get the story secondhand, credited to you.
26. Take your time. I wasn't even an account executive at 32 and further I didn't begin to know as much about this business as you do now, even with all the breaks anyone could have. No matter how able you are, older people will accept you slowly because they have learned that experience carries as high a value as genius.
27. You think you are able; I think you are able. When other people around you begin saying so, unsolicited, then you're promotable.

May 25, 1962

TO: Everyone

FROM: Wm. A. Marsteller

SUBJECT: How to Get a Raise

If anyone has written a sensible paper on the technique of getting a raise, I haven't seen it. There have been some articles written on how not to get a raise, and the whole subject has been a steady source of inspiration for unsubtle cartoons.

It is a lot easier, of course, to recite the verbotens. Then, presumably, if you avoid the pitfalls, sooner or later your

67

loving boss finds his affection for you bursting out of control and he happily raises the ante.

How you go about getting a raise at J. Walter Thompson or Harshe-Rotman, I don't know. I do, however, consider myself an expert witness in the field of getting a raise in our combine, and I see no particular reason for keeping all this delightful knowledge to myself.

First, the system. Then, how to beat it.

The system goes roughly like this:

The General Manager has final authority for all salary changes up to the executive level. There are two restrictions upon him. One is his total annual budget for salaries which he cannot exceed without getting a completely new budget past both the financial committee and the Board of Directors. The other is the general salary range of the job in question. That is to say, if two girls have approximately the same job responsibility, their salaries will be similar, but by no means necessarily the same.

Except for these restrictions, the General Manager makes the final decision, but is expected to review all pertinent data with the supervisors of the persons involved. This data includes:

1. Quality of work (accuracy, neatness, etc.).
2. Quantity of work.
3. Amount of supervision required.
4. Compatibility (relations with others, willingness to help others, etc.).
5. Attendance (absence and tardiness).
6. Potential (is there evidence of the necessary initiative, ability, educational background knowledge and personal qualifications to make eventual promotion possible?).

In the case of executive personnel, salary changes are still the responsibility of the General Manager, but subject to the final approval of an over-all compensation committee.

When a General Manager submits a request for approval of salary change, he must submit a written appraisal of each individual involved. The specific points against which he makes a written appraisal differ with whether the individual is in creative-contact work or in a service department, and whether he is doing advertising or public relations work, but in general include the following:

1. Job knowledge.
2. Judgment (business maturity, dependability, etc.).
3. Decisiveness and initiative (supervision required, initiation of projects, follow-through).
4. Planning and organization (handling of details, familiarity with work status, avoidance of overtime charges, etc.).
5. Output and costs (productivity, unbillable costs, profit consciousness, client cost consciousness).
6. Communications (adequacy of reporting to client, service departments, superiors, assistants; effectiveness at criticism; willingness to accept suggestions and to share credit).
7. Work relationships (stability, self-control, patience, tact; willingness to help others; status with suppliers and media; compatibility with others in agency).
8. Loyalty (adherence to company policies, enthusiasm, selflessness).
9. Creative ability (quality of ideas and execution, creative taste, initiator vs. imitator, personal standards of excellence).
10. Client relations (respect by clients, client communications, development of group vs. personal relationships, businesslike avoidance of expensive social involvement).
11. Management (willingness to make personal sacrifices, interest in all phases of our and our clients' business, growth of general knowledge, ability to direct others).

12. Potential (is there evidence of necessary initiative, ability, educational background, knowledge and personal qualifications to make promotion possible?)

Neither of these lists is in a sequence of relative importance, and the weight given to any point varies by the job and the experience of the individual. There is no absolute scale. Extraordinary superiority in a few categories may be enough; extraordinary deficiency in one or two key ones may be completely damning.

Now, let's talk a minute about how often people get raises and how much.

There is no set time for raises. Salary review is a continuous thing, not a quarterly or annual event. Raises may be more frequent at the lower ranges of the relative rates for a job, less frequent as a man or woman moves into higher compensation levels. Salary changes often (but not automatically) accompany changes in responsibility, permanently increased work load, transfers, etc.

Salary changes are not timed to the phases of the moon, assistance in obtaining new business (that's presumed to be a part of the job), special happiness on the part of the client for certain ads or pr work (that's what you were hired to develop), temporary peak work levels (it's that kind of a business), and other things like that.

At the same time, we do not cut salaries if we lose an account, if the client becomes temporarily unhappy with your work, if you screw up a job that costs the company money, or if you find yourself with some slack time on your hands. In fact, I only recall two cases of salary cuts in our history. One was a voluntary cut for an employee who wanted to start over in a new department. The other was me, when our profits were down a year ago and I figured if I cut my salary maybe other executives would get the hint, but that kind of hint, who can take it?

How much should a salary increase be?

Well, in general not so small that the withholding wipes it all out. Relative wage levels, time between raises, and

the reason for the raise all have something to do with it.

How do our salaries compare with other agencies?

First, most of what you read in the trade press about salaries is pure junk. As the vocational head-mechanics have pointed out for years, nobody tells the truth about his income. Some people holler poor-mouth all the time. Far more inflate their ego by inflating their salary when the surveys come in. Companies almost invariably quote salaries at the upper level on these surveys; it makes it sound even tougher to make a profit than it is.

But the AAAA collects some verified, sensible salary data every two years and redistributes it blind to member agencies. It is broken down by section of the country (San Francisco salaries are far below New York); by size of agencies (the production manager in a $150,000,000 agency has a lot more people working for him than in a $15,000,000 agency); by minimum salaries, maximum salaries and median salaries (average salaries mean nothing, since one highly-paid executive can make the average higher than the next highest salary in his job classification).

We check these carefully. We are well above the industry figures for nearly every job description in each area and in the size group in which we operate. (Comparison is by job description, not titles; titles are totally confusing in this business—some art directors can't even draw). Anyway, we do quite a bit better than our principal competitors on both median and maximum salaries, a fact you individually won't believe, but it's the truth nonetheless.

Now finally, what should you do if you think the management has forgotten you, and you are overdue for a raise?

You have three choices. You can:

1. Wait it out either (a) with resignation, or (b) with petulance. If you choose this course, the management position is that the right answer is (a).
2. Quit.
3. Talk it over with your supervisor and, eventually if you wish, with your General Manager.

The first two courses are simple, and no particular technique is required. The third is the one that calls for finesse.

To save you time and embarrassment, may I recommend *against* two approaches:

1. The "Either I get a raise or I quit" technique. My answer to this has always been and always will be, "When are you leaving?" In general, this is the Company policy since I have such a persuasive personality, but other managers do have latitude. Some who are more understanding may ask you to lay your gun on the desk and talk about it. That's up to them. Me, I just happen to think more like Matt Dillon. But it's a completely bum approach. A raise granted because of a threat is a form of dignified hijacking. Rape isn't love.

2. The "I've just had my third child and second mortgage" technique. The management position on this is that you may have as many children as you wish, but it isn't a part of the job description. If personal calamity puts you in a serious financial position, we'll try to help you out, and we have done this several times. Improvidence, however, or plain inability to live within a realistic standard, isn't a salary consideration, except in a remote and negative way.

But you are welcome, and even encouraged, to talk the matter over, if you feel you aren't properly appreciated, or if you think for some reason that no one has been looking your way lately.

If you do, put it positively. Ask what you must do to earn more. Ask your supervisor to discuss you through his eyes—and don't get mad. (Don't be embarrassed either—he'll be much more uncomfortable than you are.) Try to be objective. Try to separate your needs and desires from your relative contribution to the Company.

And try hard to believe that you aren't lost in the shuffle. Honest to God—somebody cares. Very much.

March 15, 1971

TO: Everyone

FROM: Wm. A. Marsteller

SUBJECT: Personal Agenda Positioning

Mel Anshen once wrote a very funny paper on the fine art of agenda positioning in which he suggested some rules for keeping a committee or Board or whatever from accomplishing anything.

The secret is to put unimportant items at the top of the list so that most of the time is spent on things like the paper stock for the new letterhead or whether to put rubies in the ten-year service pins. That way there'll be no time left to cover important matters and they'll be tabled until they simply disappear.

But you don't have to form a committee to achieve non-accomplishment; you can do it on your own. In fact, many people do.

If you will just start each day gradually, filling in yesterday's time sheet, checking out the paint job in the rest room, rearranging your paper clip collection and systematically reviewing what most of the office did last night, you should be able to build up a head of inertia that will last long enough so it will be too late to start anything until tomorrow.

Once I thought I was lazy and had to impose some form of self-discipline to get anything done. Now I know everyone is and it's only a matter of degree.

I observe that productive, well-organized people are happy people and people who just dawdle the days away are sour and self-accusative.

For myself, the only way I can have a satisfying day is to start out with a list of things I want to or must do. I number

them in a priority sequence and then start cleaning them off. What's left over, or added as the day goes on, is the basis for the next day's agenda. Finally things get done, more or less, or dropped. But, hopefully, it's the unimportant things that get shoved aside.

Now, isn't that a wholesome message?

February 1, 1962

TO: Everyone

FROM: Wm. A. Marsteller

SUBJECT: Professionalism

There is a fair amount of flap in the communications trade press these days about whether or not advertising and public relations are professions.

This is not a recent controversy. It was not started by Newton Minow, Earl Kinter, Vance Packard or the Potomac (nee Charles) River Boys. It has been going on as long as most of us can remember.

My observation is that it is a greater preoccupation of the insecure and immature in our business than of the established, thoughtful leaders.

Even a casual concern with semantic accuracy indicates that, by definition, advertising and public relations are not professions. There is no specialized education required, no prescribed examinations, no licensing, no taking of vows, and no enforceable and generally adopted standards of conduct, propriety and confidence defined by codes of legal responsibility and privilege.

Which is not to say there shouldn't be. Or won't ever be.

PR people take the matter of professionalism more seriously and on the whole seem more sensitive about it. Perhaps it is because of this that the public relations business takes on more of desirable characteristics of a profession

74

than does advertising generally. But it is a matter of degree only. Both are commercial occupations, and quite likely are best performed by the men and women who accept them in that context.

The lack of laws and the absence of a common code of ethics puts an unusual responsibility on the individual company or individual practitioner in advertising and public relations. We have some overtones of the recognized professions—responsibility for the welfare of others; we are privy to the confidential information of others; we are bound, if we do our job right, to build our success on the success of others, depending upon their commercial health to insure ours. If we advise carelessly, we can expose our client's stockholders and employees to financial loss or even legal damage.

So, though we practice in a business rather than a profession, we must practice professionally.

And lacking well-defined rules, we must make and then administer our own.

As a company, we have gradually developed certain principles of professionalism.

For example, we have long since quit announcing new accounts. If our client wishes to publicize the fact that he has a new agency, that is his business, as it is yours if you wish to announce that you have changed doctors. But we have decided that we will not add to the public image of the communications business as an occupation full of irresponsible, whimsical and even sordid change, by shouting of our selling success in new business. Time enough for news stories when the client, with our help, has accomplished dramatic advertising or public relations, has increased his business, and added to industry's economic strength.

Likewise, we are becoming increasingly security-minded on financial and market data entrusted to us by our clients, partly out of a growing awareness of our moral obligation, partly out of a feeling that we can eventually earn the right to handle accounts under some circumstances which are

competitive. It is interesting to note that the most highly-regarded law firms and public accountants regularly work for companies which are directly competitive, and there is no concern even though data in their possession is if anything more potentially explosive than that with which we work. Could it be that the non-competitive tradition for advertising and public relations accounts is something which grew out of the communications industry's inability to quit talking for publication after the ads are prepared and the news stories written?

We now have a company policy that we do not release news stories on the employment of new people unless they are coming in at an officer level, and we publicize promotions only when they are to a department head or officer level. The purpose is not to deflate any of our people, but to avoid adding to the flood of personnel appointments which makes our business look like a haven for the drifter, the unstable and the discontented. What company wants to put its marketing future in the hands of an agency with this appearance?

Your management's increasing involvement with the small details that insure the superior quality of our product is another evidence. (Woops! That reads like pure PR annual report talk, and we don't like anything which is pure PR talk, or pure advertising talk.) Product quality isn't just combining vigorous verbs with abrasive adjectives —it's many, many small things.

Like letters without erasure marks, well-written conference reports, layouts that are crisply executed and interestingly packaged, words spelled correctly, tidy offices, type used properly, and deadlines met, among others.

Professionalism is partly an ethical consideration.

It is also an unrelenting quest for perfection.

March 26, 1962

TO: Everyone

FROM: Wm. A. Marsteller

SUBJECT: Clients' Tastes

Within the past month, we've had at least two instances in advertising and one in public relations in which we found ourselves poles apart with a client on matters of what was or was not good for them from a communications standpoint.

This is a tricky area, and one in which perhaps a few policy pronouncements are desirable.

First, we must not do dishonest or deliberately misleading advertising or publicity, even at the expense of parting company with a client. In any such case be sure you talk the entire matter out with the General Manager of your office immediately.

However, in my experience I can think of only one case in which we were ever asked to do anything of this sort. This really isn't the problem.

Second, if we are asked to do advertising or publicity which is simply ineffective and a waste of his money, we must examine the entire problem much more carefully.

It is essential to bear in mind that the client is, after all, spending his own money. His responsibility is to his stockholders. If we find ourselves in a wide difference of opinion on style, technique, wording, media selection, or any similar area, we must present our case as best we know how, and then, after documenting our position, do as the client decides. If his decision is something we simply can't live with, or if the instances occur with regularity, then we must reappraise our position on the account. This, too, becomes a responsibility of the General Manager.

This does not mean that we should quit trying to improve our clients' tastes and understanding with respect to their advertising and publicity. Our record shows very clearly that if we do consistently good work and if we lay plans to present our recommendations in a respectful, friendly, creative way, we can make great progress in this respect. Today, we are doing truly excellent work for several clients where we once despaired of raising standards to our levels.

Remember that our work often can be judged only subjectively. In our recent meetings it was abundantly clear that we are not always wholly in agreement among ourselves on what is good or bad. But our disagreement is usually on details, rather than on the total job.

Remember, too, that advertising or publicity is not the reason our clients are in business. Their communications are only one of the many management areas that contribute to the success or failure of their companies. They must judge what we do for them in the light of what they are doing in other management areas.

Raising clients' tastes is a never-ending job, just as raising our taste and competence can never reach a final fulfillment.

So we must never become too discouraged over an occasional setback. In the life of a business—or of a businessman—there are good days and bad, and no one day seems dreadfully eventful in the final analysis. It is the constant effort to move forward and upward a little all the time that makes a business—or a businessman—great and happy.

February 14, 1963

TO: Everyone

FROM: Wm. A. Marsteller

SUBJECT: Who Left the Door Open?

Most corporations, in their collected platitudes, place themselves firmly in favor of The Open Door Policy.

This might be loosely defined as the right of any employee to march into the office of the boss and tell him how lousy things have been going lately. Even if it costs him his job.

While most corporations bleat that they, indeed, are deeply devoted to Open Doors, few really have the climate that makes such a policy work.

An Open Door Policy, to be meaningful, protects the individual against persecution or prosecution if he uses it. And that is the rub. For as a company becomes bigger it becomes more difficult for the management, however well intentioned, to prevent small-minded men and women from making life difficult for the employee who goes to a higher-up boss.

There is, of course, only one way. That is to keep small minded men and women from becoming bosses. Or, turned the other way, to make bosses understand that as managers they are in jeopardy only when they lose the respect of the managed.

We have taken out a company lifetime subscription to The Open Door Policy. We are trying to establish the kind of a climate that will make it work.

We assume that you—YOU—if you are worth a damn are sometimes going to be at cross-purposes with your boss. We assume that from time to time you will be overworked, or underworked, or fresh out of ideas, or picked upon by

79

someone who has ulcers or whose wife has ulcers, and that you are going to want to do something about it. We assume that you'll be right sometimes and wrong sometimes and sometimes no one will be able to say for sure whether you're right or wrong.

Even General Managers are sometimes wrong. Also Presidents and Board Chairmen. But they are only always wrong when they forget they are sometimes wrong.

Same with you.

If we run this company the way some of us want very much to do, you won't worry about what happens to you if you've got a bitch and you out with it. If we run this company right, you'll also understand that you won't win 'em all, and sometimes what seems oppressive to you isn't intended to be at all.

You won't sacrifice your future if you go over your boss' head with a problem. He's supposed to let you. It would be nice if you tell him you want to, however, and if he tries to stop you he's in more trouble than you are. That's one of the understandings implicit in his being a manager in this company. If he is too insecure to let you, he's not our kind of a manager. And if you really have a problem and you're too frightened to do something about it, you're not our kind either.

You don't have to swallow the company line without chewing to get a promotion or a raise around here.

You don't even have to like everyone personally, either. Even I don't. Some people are more equal than others. That's the way it is.

But we are lucky, you and I, because usually someone likes everyone, at least everyone we stable around here. So if it turns out your boss and you have little in common, other than your mutual desire to do an excellent job, that's not too important.

Just be sure that if you really have problems you don't bottle them up.

Remember, my door is always open.

Ditto the doors of our other managers, at all levels.

In spirit as well as in fact.
They'd better be.

April 21, 1965

TO: Everyone

FROM: Wm. A. Marsteller

SUBJECT: New Business

It is apparent from the reports on the annual meeting seminars that our policies on new business are rather murky in your minds, and that is giving the management all the best of it.

Perhaps this will throw a little light on what gives.

The first, and most important, fact is that we indeed do have a policy. It is in writing and is in the Policy Manual in a so-called Manager's section.

The reason the new business policy is there is because, for better or for worse, new business administration must be at a high and single level for each office. Let me give you a couple of examples why:

1. Some years ago Dick Christian and I, invited in as one of 15 agencies for a preliminary screening, walked out of a company with the account on the first contact. It was assigned to an account group, which jumped in and in three weeks we presented and got the first ads approved. A week later, a space salesman, not untypically somewhat behind current events, told one of our AE's that this company was looking for a new agency. Our AE called the Ad Manager and asked for a date. Although the Ad Manager hadn't met him, he naturally assumed we were sending him out for some purpose. So the happy little AE, bent on getting us a nice, new account, hies out

81

to our client, unrolls his charts, and begins a new business pitch. Is that any way to run an agency?

2. A handsome pr AE, running for higher office, met a guy on a commuter train and found out he was thinking about hiring a pr outfit. Our man made a half-dozen follow-up calls, telling no one, until proudly he came in with the announcement that we had a new $500 a month fee client. Hooray. Anyway, hooray today. Tomorrow, it develops, our man has promised the new client $5000 monthly service for $500 fee. Day after tomorrow, when Dun & Bradstreet report comes in (which GM would have ordered long before making deal if he'd been consulted) it develops our new client, fresh from pokey, has long-established disinterest in paying bills, among other engaging personality traits.

Well, we could give you many more, but you'd only wonder how we could ever have been so stupid, and we management don't like to be thought of as only recently nonstupid.

So we have a new business policy. It is detailed and lengthy, and just a sprinkling of tidbits from it may reassure you that we may be all wrong in our approach, but it is at least well-organized all-wrongness.

A. New business is always the responsibility of the General Manager. Only he makes the decision on what accounts are to be pursued and who will pursue them.

B. New business calls are never, never to be made by a single individual. Two or more always go.

C. No new business is taken without a prior credit check, and without analysis of the previous experience of the agencies the company had been using.

D. There is no minimum size of an account we will take, but the General Manager is expected to assure himself of its eventual profitability and growth potential.

E. In general, we will not make a presentation for a new account unless we can assure ourselves that we have at least an equal chance with any other agency, and that if we were the client in question, we would consider our agency as well qualified as any other contender.

F. We will never make a halfway presentation. Either we'll go all out or stay out.

G. Like every responsible agency that has tried it, we believe specialized new business men are a waste of money. If unsuccessful, they mirror us as unprofessional. If successful, the client wants them as the AE and they cease to be new business men.

H. We try to identify the senior men proposed for an account early in the presentation.

I. We believe in speculative work on new business—if necessary. When we get big and snooty, we may not, just like J. Walter Thompson.

J. We believe in selling the company, not a man.

K. We believe consistent advertising, sales promotion and public relations will build our business, just as it does for our clients.

L. We have lost more business because we were too young than because we were too old. Therefore, the bulk of new business is best handled by old men, like me and other father-images. We believe it is good to always bring along one or two nontired types, however, so that if the client president's son is the ad manager, he will have someone to empathize with.

M. We believe that on new business you only get one chance. Therefore, we prefer to experiment with content rather than format of presentations; we want experience for the majority of the new business team; we expect rehearsals and polish and perfection.

N. We know that we get six out of ten accounts for which we make a full-scale presentation—if they are indeed looking for a new agency. Therefore our aim

is to get a hearing before companies who want to change, not companies who want to be courteous or are simply curious.

Well, there's a lot more, but this is enough for you to disagree with at the moment.

The important thing is not whether you think what we're doing and what we believe is right or wrong; the important thing is that you know that yes, Virginia, we do have a new business policy and that hopefully, it incorporates the wisdom of both our selling successes and failures.

April 27, 1962

TO: Everyone

FROM: Wm. A. Marsteller

SUBJECT: Disappointments

Senility has no direct relationship to a specific age; it comes to different people in different degrees at different periods of life.

It comes first and most virulently, however, to egotists and Board Chairmen. There is no warning, as in the case of heart trouble, through shortness of breath. Rather, it is likely to be characterized by longness of breath.

Most particularly, however, it is accompanied by an increasing infatuation with the past. Unfortunately, the past tends to be dated and dull.

Yet, as I locate more and more of my friends among the Geritol set, I find myself pointing backwards at things that shaped our business, wondering if anyone remembers the painful and often embarrassing problems of adolescence.

For instance, I don't think we've learned much about new business presentations in the last couple of years, at least in a couple of our offices.

They say that a good batting average for an agency is one out of eight. Ours lately has been something like four out of eight.

So, hurrah?

Not necessarily.

When we win, we happily plunge into getting to work on the account, except for picking up a little scuttlebutt on how the other agencies goofed. But mostly, we don't learn anything.

But when you lose a big one, you nurse your wounds for awhile. You try to find out what you did wrong and how come the clowns from the successful agency conned such nice, intelligent-seeming people into such a poorly-considered decision.

In 1951, when the paint wasn't dry on the new sign on our door, we didn't get the Trane Company account. But *some* of us never, never, never again went into a new business presentation without *complete* rehearsal, and professional visuals, no matter how informal the prospect said he wanted things.

A couple of years later we didn't get the packaging division of Marathon paper because we couldn't show any packaging or packaging advertising. What we learned that time was that if you haven't *got* experience, that's when you do the speculative work to show how well you *could* do.

Then we didn't get the A. O. Smith account and we learned almost the biggest lessons of all: (1) If you can't make your presentation in 45 minutes, don't go; (2) If you can't talk mostly about the prospect, his customers, and his markets and marketing problems, you're too self-centered to deserve the account. Suddenly we realized that we sure had been talking about ourselves up to this point, and it sure was interesting—to us.

Then we didn't get Borg-Warner and we learned that Yale is thicker than water, as is often, Princeton. We learned that you can be the best in the House, but not get elected Speaker.

We didn't get Armour Chemical and we learned that our

30-year olds look pretty young and untried to company management that is 60, and so now we make a real advantage out of youth, rather than glossing over it. We learned to analyze what *someone else* might consider our weaknesses, and to haul them out for discussion, and then turn them into strengths.

Most of all, we learned that disappointments are temporary. You forget them. For awhile they make you mad, if you are as competitive as you ought to be to be happy in this business.

And if they make you mad enough, you'll do something about it.

When I got out of school I tried to get a job with the Buchen Company, among others. The thing I really was mad about at Walther Buchen was that he filled the two vacancies at the time with a couple of boys whose papas were presidents of companies that looked like Buchen prospects.

I decided that if you can't join 'em, lick 'em.

We haven't always been successful, and I'm not so mad any more, but we're still trying.

And we don't confine that to Buchen. It's fun to beat Thompson, too. Or any agency.

And that's not unprofessional. It's the drive for success that translates into a burning desire not just for the best clients, but also, on their behalf, for the best advertising.

March 7, 1967

TO: Everyone

FROM: Wm. A. Marsteller

SUBJECT: The Billings Shell Game

Each year, as the ides of March approach, *Advertising Age* labors loudly and spews out an issue dedicated

to a ranking of agencies according to their billing, real or imaginary.

For the first 14 years of our corporate existence we threw their questionnaire away.

We felt it was preposterous to jumble the likes of J. Walter Thompson, which gets 85 to 90 per cent of its income from commissions, with medical, industrial, financial, agricultural and other special types of agencies (not to mention agencies whose only specialty is small accounts) who get half or more of their income from fees, mark-ups, retainers, sales promotion and various special projects.

The only true measure of an agency's size is, of course, its total income, or, perhaps, its number of employees.

Now on media—space or time—income is 15 per cent of billing. Therefore a $100,000,000 agency which is almost entirely dependent upon commissions really has total sales of about $15,000,000.

The bigger agencies don't like to talk about themselves that way. They are uncomfortable about the fact that underneath it all—for all its importance and for all its publicity—the advertising agency business is really made up of quite small corporations.

So it has been customary to "capitalize" income into billings to have a common standard by which to compare agencies. You capitalize income by multiplying it by 6⅔. So, as we have often pointed out, $15,000 in fees is exactly the same income as $100,000 in commissionable space.

For 14 years we didn't submit figures to *Ad Age,* so they published their own estimate. In our first years, perhaps because we were noisier than the youthful should be, *Ad Age* generously gave us credit for being bigger than we were. Nice.

As the years went by and we grew we also became more reticent and adopted a policy some years ago of not announcing new accounts, a policy which may or may not be outmoded but is still in effect. So in due time *Ad Age* was underestimating our relative size by quite a bit. Ouch.

A year ago we decided to give *Ad Age* our income.

Then they would capitalize it and we'd be where we belonged. *Ad Age* corrected their estimates and presumably everyone was happy.

Except, of course, some of our old-time competitors who hadn't been growing so much and hadn't really been aware that we had, though they could have gotten a clue from total employees.

Well, this year we once again sent *Ad Age* our income figure—$7,046,000, as you will remember from the annual meetings. If you chose to multiply that by 6⅔ you will see that our domestic and foreign billing capitalizes to just short of $47,000,000. *Ad Age* so published it.

However, they employed a new element in their rankings this year. They said that $100,000 of commissionable billings was $100,000 but that $15,000 of fees (which is exactly the same income) was only $15,000.

In their listing a couple of weeks ago they overlooked the fact that about half our income is from fees, retainers, mark-ups and collateral. But you can bet some of our envious competitors didn't and apparently the howls were horrendous.

So *Ad Age* revalued us today at $27,000,000 or thereabouts which they got by the ingenious, if totally irrational, method of multiplying half our income by 6⅔, and then adding the other half without doctoring.

Ad Age says they adopted this new method because that's what the Census Bureau does. Right there they should have been put on guard.

So, you see, it seems that half our income is worth six times the other half.

I saw our landlord in Chicago the other noon and asked if he'd take the rent payment half in $1.00 dollars and the other half in 15¢ dollars. He is very conservative. He said "no." He said he liked all dollars to be the same.

The whole thing is so stupid, so illogical, so childish it is perhaps not worth all this belaboring except that people take these rankings seriously. Any careful reader of the supporting data on the agencies knows that most of the

billings figures for the medium and small agencies are kited, that employment figures have no relationship to income (which, of course, they should), and that adding fees and billings together is totally invalid by any accounting standard you could apply.

Last week, a client for whom we spend about $700,000 in commissionable media signed a contract agreeing to pay us a supplemental fee of $60,000 a year to cover the excessive costs of many variations of each ad, translations, etc. That fee is the same income as if we'd gotten another $400,000 account, but *Ad Age* says no, it's only $60,000.

But what difference, really. If we run our business with one set of figures—income—we'll know what we're doing. We'll know that when a client pays us $60,000, that's what we have to work with.

We are disturbed only because some of your friends won't understand *Ad Age's* "correction" which seems to reduce our billing from $46,000,000 to $27,000,000 in a year, incidentally, in which we had a nearly 30 per cent growth in income.

But perhaps the most appalling aspect of this messy situation is the apparent lack of understanding of the economics of the advertising agency business by the publication commonly accepted as the principal medium devoted to the advertising business. To equate a dollar of income with a dollar of billings is plainly ridiculous—a quality tolerable in some but one not expected of a publication with the reputation of *Advertising Age.* Hopefully, their own staff members will attend their very next seminar on agency finances.

May 15, 1963

TO: Everyone

FROM: Wm. A. Marsteller

SUBJECT: Confidential Information

Recently, for the first time in this business's history, one of our employees was guilty of a security leak that seriously embarrassed the client, and it goes without saying, put us in an extremely difficult position.

The penalty for such indiscretion can be only one thing: immediate dismissal.

In our business we are privy to many confidential matters relating to client plans and operations. Our clients assume that we are to be trusted. If we are to be given the information we need to do our job properly, we must solicit such trust.

There are two ways a confidence can be broken. One is deliberate, such as providing a friendly space salesman or editor with inside information to make his job easier. It is unnecessary to comment on such a practice. If any public relations or advertising man is guilty of such business immorality, he should not only be dismissed but subsequent employers should be warned.

A more understandable, though no less dangerous, form of indiscretion is simple blabbing. This business is a natural for gregarious people who like to talk about their work, their experiences, their associations. Most of this is completely harmless. Sometimes, if good judgment is used, it can be most useful. But it takes business maturity to talk about specific clients and stay away from all types of confidential information. A better way is to avoid client discussions completely.

Especially if you're having a drink at the time.

At a time when we, among a few responsible agencies, have been arguing that the old verboten against competitive accounts is archaic, carelessness with client confidences is especially unforgivable. We have been taking the position that we are as dependable as public accountants or attorneys who often handle competing accounts with strict professional adherence to the strictest of confidence.

We simply cannot be careless.

If you are a jingle-jaws you are in the wrong business with the wrong company.

October, 1970

TO: Everyone

FROM: Wm. A. Marsteller

SUBJECT: Political Accounts

During this political season, I have been asked several times why we don't handle political accounts.

It certainly isn't because we have not been asked. In the last four or five years, we have shied away from a variety of requests in several offices and from both parties.

As a matter of policy, we have concluded that most political candidates don't represent the kind of clients for whom we wish to work. There are some good reasons.

In the first place, handling a political campaign is highly disruptive to the regular conduct of business. For a relatively short period of time, it demands excessive attention, puts people under great pressure, and undoubtedly short-changes regular clients who pay our bills year in and year out.

Second, we are uneasy about putting our employees in a position of working on political accounts when their ideology may be totally opposed to that of the candidate. This applies not only to the account and creative staff but to

service department personnel as well, who not infrequently in a political campaign are expected to work all night or right through several consecutive weekends, often for somebody they abhor.

Third, the history of agency-political relations is studded with financial difficulties. As emotions rise and panic sets in toward the end of a campaign, caution and budgets go out the window and many an agency has found itself eating the final costs of a campaign with no recourse against a candidate, his party, or, more likely, a spurious committee that goes out of business the minute the polls close.

Finally, and most important of all, political advertising is very often dirty advertising. An awful lot of what I have heard and seen during the recent political campaign is far below the ethical standards of this agency.

It is especially galling to me to see some of the political advertising for men who have been so critical of commercial advertising, often attacking it as untruthful or at best misleading and distorted. These same politicians, working on their own behalf, employ people whose business morals are well below those of most good agencies and then encourage them to produce advertising that, if it were for a corporation or for a product, would be in trouble with the FTC, the FCC, the FDA, the Department of Justice, and a half dozen assorted agencies and commissions.

It seems to me that it might not be a bad idea to play back some of the campaign tapes during the assorted witch-hunting investigations of advertising.

On rare occasions we have made an exception and handled political advertising. During this past campaign, for the second time, we have been the agency for Houston I. Flournoy, Controller of the State of California. Our understanding with him and with our people is that we will turn over no one to the campaign full time, that no one needs to work on the campaign if he doesn't wish to, that we have cash in advance before we make media commitments, and that we never do any advertising for him that isn't completely truthful and in good taste. What Mr. Flournoy's

ultimate future in politics will be, heaven only knows. Hopefully, it will be good. It would be reassuring to see an ethical and honest man make it big in an arena where more than one standard seems to apply.

January 15, 1971

TO: Everyone

FROM: Wm. A. Marsteller

SUBJECT: The Outlook

So now comes all the apple-crapple about what kind of a year 1971 is going to be.

Most of the people you see quoted either don't know any more than you do, or are making statements to push their own interests, like politicians, publishers and professors.

In our business, it is very hard for anyone to be publicly pessimistic, although if you read the outlook roundup stories for enough years, you come to understand the double-speak used for these gropings into the future.

For instance, one agency president is quoted as viewing 1971 with "cautious optimism." Translation: "If we have a good new business year, we will just about offset reduced budgets."

Another sees a "firming up of budgets from last year" that means he doesn't expect to be down much more than 10 per cent overall. And the frequently used statement that we'll have "a stronger second half" means that, on the whole, the outlook for year after next is a little better.

Our 1970, as we'll soon be reporting at the annual meetings, was lacklustre to say the least. But our volume was up and the last two quarters were better from a profit standpoint, and our budgets for 1971 are an improvement, if still below our best.

93

Actually, external business conditions are only a part of it. In every period of slow business some companies do well, gaining ground faster than in good times.

And there's nothing in a business pinch to make us do bad ads or pedestrian pr. Quite the contrary.

We've had an excellent new business year, right through all our offices. I have a hunch we'll look back in a few years and conclude that tight business was a particular opportunity for a company like ours.

December 12, 1971

TO: Everyone

FROM: Wm. A. Marsteller

SUBJECT: Little Things, Like Expense Accounts and Smoke Rings

Lately and for the first time in a long time, we've had to pull the strings on a few expense accounts. I hear some people think this is a tight company.

Hooray.

I'm in this deal on the same basis as you. I get the same proportionate share of the profit sharing plan as you do, if you've been here long enough to qualify, and I know that 50 cents of every dollar of profit, after certain minimums, goes right into that pot.

I like profit.

I like profit sharing.

So, I hope the company will continue to be businesslike about expenses.

But that isn't the main reason for asking our controller to make fish eyes at expense accounts. Not just to save money. Rather, to build good client relationships.

Overentertaining is dangerous:

1. It is habit-forming and once started, you are stuck forever with entertaining certain people, even when their jobs change; and at a certain standard, even when you outgrow the thrill of rich desserts.
2. Client *managements* usually don't like it. They become suspicious that somebody may be bought off, and so we are putting the people we entertain in jeopardy as well as ourselves.
3. It looks like a substitute for performance. Entertainment won't save a bum job, but a good job doesn't need to be supported with elaborate entertainment.
4. It interferes with getting the job done. No one, not even me, works well after a sodden lunch, or looks well after continuous after-hours hosting.
5. It puts us in the class with Madison-Avenue type agencies, and all the unpleasant connotations of Martini Row.
6. It puts business on a social plane, where it doesn't belong.

So what is this—an order to cut out entertaining?

Decidedly not. It is a plea to use judgment. Think about the perils as well as the pleasures. Entertain, yes; with good taste, at infrequent intervals, in such a manner that you wouldn't care if the President of the client company audited your expense account.

* * *

The other day I went to a presentation where one of our client's AM's talked to a group with a cigarette dangling out of his mouth, flipping ashes on the carpet, and the rest, while he spoke.

I'm getting old. I was upset.

Of course, we don't do such unmannerly things. There are too many fine people who find such performances distasteful.

I couldn't help thinking of the story Nels Bond, of McGraw-Hill, told about a young *BUSINESS WEEK* salesman in Pittsburgh. That was the day I got the message and quit smoking in clients' or prospects' offices unless they offered me a cigarette first.

Seems the young salesman and Nels called on a woman ad manager in Pittsburgh. The young man lit a cig, looked for an ash tray and there was none. He held the burned match and peered around, but the AM didn't bat an eyelash. Came ash time, the YM was getting embarrassed. Finally used cuff of his trousers. Repeat. Ditto. Now cig is a half-inch long. Carpeted floor.

Crush into rug? Ask for non-existent tray? Hold up two fingers and leave? Eat hot butt?

The YM made a quick decision. He opened the window and threw it out, but when he did the papers on the lady's desk blew all over the floor.

We fade out on the YM, making first sales call, and boss, swearing softly, crawling around on floor trying to put things back together.

December 27, 1961

TO: Everyone

FROM: Wm. A. Marsteller

SUBJECT: Poor Music

When I was a kid, every Saturday morning I worked in my father's grocery store until noon, for which I got 30¢.

That was the price of a ticket at the Saturday matinee at the Orpheum Theatre, which had a six-act vaudeville bill.

I know what killed vaudeville. I was there.

It was the one-man band.

There were a lot of such acts in vaudeville. A guy came out with a collection of instruments, many homemade, and

he blew and pounded and swung and hollered like a cool fool, and the effect was pretty bad. I knew it even then.

One-man bands never had star billing; they got by because they were cheap, they filled a spot in the show, and they made good acts look better by comparison.

I never saw a one-man band that did any one thing very well.

* * *

One-man bands have killed a lot of other things.
Like advertising agencies.
And PR firms, too.

* * *

We are anti one-man bands.

One-man bands are cheap from an agency standpoint. You cut down on salaries. You don't need much supervision. You pay on a percentage of billing and, if it falls, your salary commitment falls. You cut down on conferences. You cut down on research. You don't have to worry about promotions; a guy wants more money, he goes out and tries to hustle more business. Then tries frantically to handle it.

In such an agency people get opinionated, selfish, suspicious, and they never grow much intellectually.

And the campaigns (more often just "ads") they produce could come from a dozen different agencies.

But it *is* cheap.

Only trouble is, the results show it.

So we don't want one-man bands.

We don't want guys thinking their judgment and creative and marketing skills are so well developed they don't need both pre- and post-criticism. In this business no one is that sure-footed.

So when you write copy, we think someone else with guts ought to criticize it. You don't have to take all suggestions, but you ought to submit to them. PR copy or advertising copy; it's all the same.

Likewise layouts. Or type selection.

Or marketing plans. *Especially* marketing plans.

97

Ask for creative meetings on your accounts. PR or advertising.

To ask for help and suggestions is not a confession of weakness; it's a demonstration of strength.

Only the inferior person is afraid to expose his lack of knowledge; only the basically knowledgeable seeks more knowledge.

You may play trumpet beautifully, but you'll sound better accompanied. If you learn to use an accompanist.

The best campaigns we've ever done were the work of many people; not just one.

For every one, we have at least three people who can say, with honesty, "I did it." Good.

The worst campaigns, the worst publicity jobs, are almost always the work of some single, easily-identifiable individual, who didn't have the courage, or the humility, or the good sense to ask for help or criticism.

They used to knight guys just for putting a crummy coat down in a mud puddle to help some dame keep from getting her dirty feet even dirtier.

It's a lousy analogy, but I had it left over.

November 2, 1962

TO: Everyone

FROM: Wm. A. Marsteller

SUBJECT: Miscellaneous Boy Scout-Type Mouthings

Bill Blair, Sales Manager of *Harper's* and the *Atlantic,* writes:

"Like other magazines, we give occasional lunch presentations. We don't know whether other magazines share with us the no-show problem; people who accept and then, without notification, don't come. It's a problem we

have learned to cope with since the defections run a fairly steady 15 per cent—which may be a magic number, at that. But an interesting observation emerges: the higher a person's status, the more punctilious he is about fulfilling his engagements."

He's talking about other agencies, we hope. Surely no one in this company has such boorish manners as to accept a luncheon invitation and then simply not show. Telephone service is readily available to any publisher who runs a presentation and you are expected, as a matter of civilized courtesy, to let him know if your plans must be changed.

*   *   *

In Burson-Marsteller there seems to be some kind of a rhubarb about what constitutes a "feature" article in the monthly box score of accomplishments.

Ho hum.

Definitions are so boring.

When a public speaker starts out by saying, "First, let's see what Webster says," my advice is, second, head for the nearest bar. You have just been given the first clue in a verbal scavenger hunt from a man who is about to do his thinking out loud, hoping that the trail will lead to philosophical treasures. Only it never does. It will finally run out in some well-trampled cabbage patch.

I'll tell you what is a feature story. It is an *Iron Age* cover, an appearance on *Today,* two pages in *Business Week,* an AP item that produces 200 clips, a picture in *Life,* a speaking slot at the national convention of the *Asme,* or three pages of "how to" in *Oil & Gas Journal.* Get enough of those and neither you nor anyone else will quibble about the definition of features.

I had a college textbook in sociology which had a wonderful definition. I memorized it and saved it for instant use at cocktail parties, political rallies, Bartok recitals and learned discussions about finite definitions. It said: "The aim of socialization is the inculcation of that social al-

truism which is the antithesis of egocentricity and its whole array of criminogenic consequences."

On the other hand, when Red Grange was asked to define the purpose of football, he said, "Scoring touchdowns."

* * *

There was one of those questionnaires in the mail today asking what advertising and general business magazines I read, how often, which I prefer, and all that pap.

Nearly every time I get one of these I have to check off darned near every magazine on the sheet. Scotty Sawyer, who knows about such things, says the same thing can be said of nearly every one of our more highly paid people. He also says that this isn't so among some of our juniors. He's too kind a man to suggest that it might also be true of a few seniors.

When does a man become successful enough in the communications business to find it unnecessary to read the trade and business press regularly and in depth?

I can't answer. I always have; I still do.

But I guess it's different with some people or they wouldn't keep making these surveys.

Speeches on the World of Communications

For many years, Bill Marsteller spoke and wrote on a wide variety of subjects ranging from basic business principles to the specifics of advertising creativity.

Here are some of the most widely quoted and reprinted of those statements.

Communications

Bill Marsteller never thinks of himself as an advertising man but rather as a "communications" man. A number of his talks and memos were addressed to the problem of understanding and the barriers heredity and environment erect against clarity.

ON THE PROBLEM OF UNDERSTANDING

My business, as you have been reminded, is communications.

Thank God, communications isn't a disease, because we know so little about it.

Everybody talks, few hear.

A lot of people write, fewer read, almost no one understands.

My office in New York is a block from the United Nations. There are always pickets, and they come in all sizes and all states of unwash. They shout "Ban the Bomb," or "Get out of Vietnam," or "Recognize Castro." Those are their words, but what do they mean?

Who is it that is to ban the bomb? How?

Whom do they want to get out of Vietnam?

Recognize Castro? You'd recognize Castro anywhere, by the beard and the smell. What do they mean, "Recognize Castro?"

How do you communicate with them?

Do you go up to them and say, "I don't quite understand you. What is it you wish done?" They yell back at you "Imperialist! Warmonger! Fink!" And the New York Police Department says to you, "Move along; leave 'em alone." And then the pickets scream, "Police brutality!"

In a dozen communities today there are pickets parading,

chanting "Jim Crow Must Go!" Yet a recent study made by a major publication, trying to find out how to get through to Negro readers, shows that nearly 70 per cent of the Negroes studied—and nearly 50 per cent of whites—couldn't even vaguely describe what "Jim Crow" meant. A prime objective of the Negro leaders is equal opportunity—housing and employment in particular, and specifically, by their words, equal opportunity for white-collar jobs. But the same study of comprehension shows that 80 per cent of the Negroes demonstrating for white-collar jobs couldn't describe what a white-collar job meant.

Do you understand what your own children are saying to you? Do you really communicate with them? Or are you verbally picketing each other?

"Don't stay out too late."

What does it mean? You think it means, "You will feel better tomorrow and do better in school if you get proper rest." Your kid thinks it means his father is observing the ritual of parenthood, like giving the sign to get into lodge meeting. It has no literal meaning to him, except perhaps as an implied threat.

We can send a rocket to the moon, we can orbit a man around the earth a dozen times in a day, we can make thread out of coal, and prevent polio with a pill, and yet we can't communicate.

With no effort at all we could blow Cambodia right off the map. In the face of this certain knowledge, Cambodians stone our embassy simply because we have not been able to find a way to hold out our hands and say, "We want to be your friend," and make them understand what we mean.

Everyone knows that certain words and certain ideas simply do not translate, one language to another. What we are less conscious of is that there are just as many, or even more, that don't translate within the same language from one social or economic or ethnic group to another.

For instance, Negro leaders constantly remind us that if you have never been a Negro, you can never know how a Negro feels and thinks. Johnny Johnson, the publisher of

Ebony, says the Negro really doesn't orient to the white middle class. He looks down on the white *lower* class, sure in himself that if he were white he wouldn't be trapped at *that* cultural level. He vastly envies the upper class white— *upper* class in the economic sense—and buys Cadillacs, custom-made shirts, tailor-made suits, and if he breaches the white color line in a restaurant, goes to the best. It is not unnatural. As a race the Negro has driven the boss' Cadillac, washed his boss' custom-made shirt, pressed his tailor-made trousers. He has no way, in most cases, to relate to the solid middle-class white.

Whites in the East are appalled that Congressman Adam Clayton Powell, whose private life is somewhat noxious, can still attract 2,000 Negroes to Harlem's Abyssinian Baptist Church any Sunday he chooses to evade the process servers and preach. A New York newspaper questioned some of the congregation about what they thought about their preacher's self-indulging social life. Their viewpoint was summed up by one who said, "Man, that cat sure do swing."

Do we really understand him? Do we understand the admiration Powell's congregation has for him in the face of his doubtful moral code? Do we understand the obvious devotion to a man who has flaunted established white laws and morals and come away without punishment—even with new prestige and power?

As a livelihood, I commit advertising. It is a very difficult form of communications. When I was a newspaper reporter, like most writers I wrote for my own understanding, and possibly for the understanding of my editor. If a vast portion of the people who read what I wrote didn't understand everything the way I wanted them to, there was no feedback.

In advertising, however, you soon become sensitive to the reality that the hardest question to answer in the English language is "Do I make myself clear?" because there is no way for the person to whom you are talking to know what kind of clear you are trying to make yourself. You are asking, "Do you understand my ideas as I understand them?"

and about the only way to find out is by asking him to play back his interpretation of what you have just said. This is no way to win friends. It is another way of saying, "You don't understand me," which Dale Carnegie said could be abbreviated to "You dope!"

In advertising, the playback is usually sales. Because there is a commercial, profit-based reason for getting the idea across, advertising is pre-tested and post-tested and people are asked in many studies to tell what they just read or just learned in their own words.

Copywriters are consistently astounded on how they are misunderstood.

It is very, very hard to be clear.

The biggest barrier to effective communications—of business to government and labor, of the old to the young, of the haves to the have-nots, of the southerner to the northerner, of Sybil Burton to Elizabeth Taylor—is not language or vocabulary, but attitude.

Hardening of the attitude starts long before hardening of the arteries. Our physical and philosophical postures are a product of both our heredity and environment.

We are born Democrats or Republicans or Catholics or Presbyterians or agnostics or whatever. Though I know of no statistics on the matter, I think simple observation shows that only a small segment of our population squanders its inherited religious and political estate. In fact, it is common that early attitudes in these matters, handed down from generation to generation, are hardened by specific education. I believe one of the reasons that there are fewer defections among Catholics, compared for instance with Presbyterians, is the much more intensive development of the inherited thought-strain through religious education.

It is popular these days to think that the mission of education is not to pass on accepted knowledge but to teach the ability to think. Yet, of course, the fact is that much, if not most, early education actually cripples our ability to think freshly.

Two plus two equals four. Two plus two equals four. Say

it again: two plus two equals four. Now tell me, Johnny: what is two and two? Could it possibly be five? It is un-thinkable; you have had it drummed into you so long that your mind won't let you approach the possibility that maybe two and two isn't four, just like, it turns out, the world isn't flat.

It is hard for an uneducated man to communicate because he lacks the words with which to do it; it is hard for an educated man to communicate because he thinks there is so much that needs no communication because it is accepted fact. But is it?

These days we have people making much use of the old, old communications technique of mass demonstrations. Demonstrations, in one form or another, have been with us through most of recorded history. They are newly popu-lar, I think, because many of our problems are so complex today that we have segments of our population completely frustrated in their ability to explain how they feel. So they resort to the communications refuge of the little child and shout, "I hate you." Or, perhaps, "You hate me," which is the same thing.

These demonstrations, as you have observed, offer only slogans, not solutions. They are manifestations of hardened attitudes. There are no liberals or reactionaries on these picket lines; they are all reactionaries. They are defending a position, not persuading a population.

Any successful advertising man learns early that you move neither products nor minds by attack. You do it by facts, logic, attractive presentation, by bending the cliché, so it's still comfortably recognizable, but twisted enough so you see a new idea.

"Think Small," said Volkswagen and all kinds of people re-examined their old attitude about the size of automobiles. Volkswagen had a choice. They could have made the same point by picketing and rock-throwing. They could have said, "Americans are Status Seekers." "Don't be a sucker for Detroit," or even "Ban the Chevrolet," or, "Fords are Not Good For You."

What is there we can do about all this?

Well, as I said, complex problems need more than slogans for answers.

As far as the demonstrations are concerned, I think the reaction of thinking men is not difficult. I think we need to control them only to the extent of maintaining law and order and property rights, and then put them in their proper context—as a primitive, self-dramatizing communications mechanism of the intellectually immature.

A quick illustration by way of support: the same groups that turned the University of California into ugly bickering among students, faculty and the administration, having made their point took up their picketing immediately again, this time on behalf of their right to be vulgar and obscene, a childish reaffirmation of their obvious immaturity.

But even though I suppose it seems I am being hard on education as a mechanism to bring about the kind of communication that begets the understanding that begets peace, I do not mean it that way.

For the fact is that it is only the educated, only the intellectual, who have the tools of words and the turn of mind to make even the first strides.

It seems to me that a great threat to the ability of the university to educate, not to recite, but to reconsider, lies in the increasing urbanization of education.

Urbanization does a strange thing to people. In the midst of cultural plenty, surrounded by museums, the theatre, music and recreation they become provincial to a degree no small town citizen could even comprehend. Having everything at hand, they go nowhere. Having every kind of an ethnic, business, religious, political, and philosophical group at hand, they retreat tightly to their own as if they were frightened at the prospect of challenge of their comfortably worn ideas.

In a highly urbanized society, the banker is most comfortable with bankers, accountants with accountants, and

professors with professors, usually in the same discipline. For instance, at Harvard you soon learn that the teachers of humanities do not associate with the teachers at the Graduate School of Business.

This is ghetto living and ghetto thinking of the worst kind that breeds the worst conformity of all—the conformity of belief.

Closed-mindedness—intolerance—is the biggest threat to the continued growth and peace of the nation. Intolerance in the uneducated is unfortunate but not frightening because it can be treated and, even if not cured, at least it is not likely to be contagious.

But intolerance among the educated is intolerable. And intolerance comes from narrowed perspectives. Intolerance comes from the inbreeding of economists to economists, doctors to doctors, rich women to rich women, Jew to Jew, Polish to Polish, and from the isolation that soon makes them unseeing of the diverse human thought and conduct around them.

Conversely, therefore, tolerance and understanding comes from resisting temptation to slip into tightly-knit little units that create a false set of priorities and tend to shield us from the totality of the society as a whole. No one is immune. And all the cant in the world, all the protestations about liberality and open-mindedness don't hide the truth.

The truth is that developing real tolerance and understanding is an unattainable accomplishment in the absolute. It can only be an unending search through unceasing self-examination.

Management Principles

In late 1961, Bill Marsteller made a speech, "On The Pursuit of Excellence." With the same title, over the next three or four years he spoke before perhaps a dozen advertising agency and business groups. The first of these talks, and one typical of the subsequent speeches with the same subject, follows. The second, by the way, was before a group of architects in New York City.

ON THE PURSUIT OF EXCELLENCE

Before nightfall, I would guess, five or ten thousand depressingly mediocre advertisements will be rushed into production in advertising agencies across the country. They will be honest ads, and they will not be offensive to good taste, unless, like nature, you abhor a vacuum.

Today, hundreds—maybe thousands—of vapid, bland, trite and tired television and radio commercials will be approved for exposure to an increasingly unimpressed and therefore unresponsive audience.

None of them, probably, will be attacked by the non-advertising critics of advertising, and it is highly unlikely that a single one of them will wind up before the AAAA-ANA Committee for Improvement of Advertising Content, nor will they ever come to the attention of the Federal Trade Commission or any other regulatory body.

Yet, in my opinion, here is the core of the problem of the advertising industry.

We have set up the machinery, voluntarily, to deal with malpractice in our industry. And if our policing falls down it will be done for us by government.

Dishonesty we can deal with quickly and positively. Offensiveness and bad manners, while more subjective, carry social penalties in advertising as they do in any other phase of civilized life.

But dullness, toothlessness, emptiness—aren't these, too, frauds of a sort?

Advertising, weak or strong, charming or churlish, is created by people. And therefore the problem, if you will agree with me that there is one, must spring from people and the way they use their talents.

The worst of it is that tonight, perhaps a hundred thousand communications people will go home without the slightest sense of guilt for having irretrievably thrown away another day of their lives, without having made a real effort to translate their unique and personal ability into a truly creative contribution to the business they have chosen.

This sounds harsh and exaggerated, and perhaps it is. When you are worried it is easy to lose a sense of proportion. And I am worried.

This is not a formula speech. Still, having viewed with alarm, I must in all conscience point with pride.

For also today, here and there—in New York, in Chicago, Los Angeles, and maybe Jacksonville or Albany, or Des Moines or Zanesville—some fine advertising was produced.

And somewhere there are some men and women going home reasonably content whether it was payday or not, because they did something of value; they discharged an obligation to themselves.

But their number, I am persuaded, is miserably small.

The whole thing is a reflection on our business, and probably even more on our national state of mind.

I'd like, for a few minutes, to think with you again of some old fashioned principles of human dignity, ambition and responsibility that seem to be going out of style. I'd like to enlist as many of you as I can in a campaign to rebuild the values of restless striving and the satisfying selfishness of superiority.

You know, the question is not whether you or I or any of the people in our companies want excellence. We all do, of course. The question is: how much will we pay for it?

We confuse ourselves with our image of what excellence is. Because we make awards, because we single out the 100 Best Advertisements, or the Ten Best Commercials of the

year, we tend to think of excellence as a brilliantly executed inspiration.

But this is all wrong. Excellence is not reserved for the inordinately talented; excellence, I am convinced, springs not so much from stark inventiveness as from clarity of purpose and attention to detail.

I think this is very close to our biggest problem in advertising.

I think you and I can nurture excellence in our business if we painstakingly set about creating and keeping the climate in which good advertising will flourish.

How do we do this? I should like to suggest a platform under which we are trying very hard, in our own little, groping way, to bury mediocrity in our business.

First of all, we are trying to put our most creative people in the most sensitive spots in the company—those that carry the most prestige and the most money.

Second, while we are, of course, trying to hire the best people we possibly can, as every agency I've ever heard of is also doing, we are at the same time trying to eliminate from our staff those of low ambition and limited ability.

Third, we are trying to be articulate to our people about the work they are doing. We praise publicly and criticize quietly, but we are trying to let all our people realize that what they are doing is being judged.

Fourth, we have only one set of standards—all the way from getting to work on time through the writing of conference reports and including preparation of advertising itself, and those standards are equally binding on management and non-management people of every station.

For a few minutes, let's look at each of them.

First, again, the matter of making bosses out of our most creative people. This is all wrong according to most of the books on personnel and management guidance. The best writer isn't the best manager; the best artist is perhaps antisocial; the production man who has a real deepdown love for type designs and who can see beauty in fine offset printing whether the illustration is beautiful or not per se, is

undoubtedly not the best man under the pressures of high-speed departmental work flow. Anyway this is what we are told. You know how this philosophy goes and the odds are you believe this.

I don't. Or at least, I *do* believe this:

There are a few really fine writers who are good businessmen; there are a few artists who are truly gregarious and responsive to client motivations; there are production men with both a sense of urgency and a sense of beauty.

So, if these people *do* exist, in however limited quantities, why shouldn't they work with *us?*

So we are preoccupied with filling in the gaps (and needless to say, none of us is without them) in the best people we have; finding those who may be elsewhere and then keeping them happy though harried.

So task number one is giving the excellent people the excellent jobs.

The second point is pruning—cutting away the weak limbs so that there's more room and more light for the strong ones to grow.

This is one of the hardest jobs in any business, I think, and it seems to be worse in advertising than in many others.

We hire a man with hope, persecute him with procrastination and fire him with fear. And it's wrong—it's bad business and immoral.

Unfortunately, ineptitude is as contagious as excellence, and just as your brightest man polishes everyone he works with to some degree, so does the friction of contact with your dullest man, just a little, erode the strength of everyone with whom he works. Further, we rationalize (I hope honestly) that if we can't give a man opportunity, we penalize him doubly by also denying him his freedom by keeping him around.

So task number two is: opportunity to everyone. In our company if he seems to have the seeds of excellence by our definition; elsewhere, if he does not.

The third point has to do with recognition, positive or negative, of the work being done.

Dr. Melvin Anshen of Columbia, who has worked on

manpower development with many of our leading companies, says that what your and our employees want most of all is to know how they stand. He says that silence is one of the greatest inhibiters of creative drive. Creative people, he believes, respond strongly to praise, but most of all, they want not to be ignored. Routine work, routine advertising assignments, cease to become routine when they are noticed.

This is a management job. First of all, any of us in agencies with responsibility for management at any level must want excellence very badly ourselves. We must turn the light on it brightly when we discover it. We must not let ourselves become so busy in client contact, or financial analysis or other matters as to forget that our product is people. Two-thirds of our costs are the people in our employ. When we waste our people's talents we are wasting our own money.

In a manufacturing plant, the scrap heap is only rusting metal cuttings or porous castings or decomposing chemicals. In our business, the scrap heap is people, and therefore far more precious. Our moral responsibility is much greater.

If we would worry more about our people—take far more interest in each job that they do—we would raise our quality dramatically. A sound and imperishable sales-advertising idea, I need hardly remind you, is the finest hedge of all against client turnover.

It is the fourth point—that of a single set of high standards for all our people and for all that we do, that I firmly believe is the greatest influence on what will happen to the advertising industry in this country.

If a dishonest advertisement is placed by an agency, some agency head is responsible for letting it happen. Through his lack of courage to face facts with his client— the fact that it is simply bad business for all concerned— he has demonstrated to his employees that they are part of a weak, opportunistic enterprise. Any inborn appetite for excellence is soon checked.

If advertising which is in poor taste is placed by **an**

agency, the management brands itself to its employees as boorish and insensitive and servile and this, too, stifles excellence.

But as I said at the start, this kind of case exists so seldom, and is so quickly purified by the stream of public exposure, as Jim Young puts it, that such gross abuses cannot long continue.

Our failure, as managers, I think, is in downgrading our efforts by inattention and by multiple standards.

At this point I want to tell you a story. I include names and details to make the record complete.

One day last spring, a former Vice President and Account Executive of our agency came to visit me. He had retired last November 1. His name is Lucien Brouillette. He had been with two other agencies before he joined us ten years ago when our agency was founded. His whole career has been in advertising.

He was getting ready to take a six-month trip to Europe, and he looked fine and happy and enthusiastic. He fell to talking about his years in advertising, and laughing about some of the problems that had now misted away into the distance, and finally I asked him what his greatest satisfaction had been.

He reminded me of the case of the Roura Iron Works, a small Detroit company which is still our client.

About seven years ago, the president of this company walked into our Chicago office and asked for the manager of new business. We have never had such a person. I was out, and the switchboard operator, not knowing what to do, called Lucien.

Mr. Roura explained that his company, a parts fabricator for plants around Detroit, had developed a self-dumping hopper which went on the front of fork-lift trucks. He had sold a few around Detroit, and customers liked them. An editor of one of the materials handling magazines had seen one, sent one of the space salesmen to call on Mr. Roura and he convinced him that they should advertise. He then sent him to us because we happened to have several accounts in materials-handling industries.

Lucien found out Roura had sold only a few hoppers, by word of mouth, and was completely unsophisticated in the usual sales-advertising routines. But he became convinced that they had a good product, and he then convinced Roura he could spend $15,000 on advertising the next year, and finally he persuaded us we should take his little account.

This was the complex problem—only $15,000, no distribution, an unknown company, inadequate facilities to build demonstration models for nation-wide showings, a new product.

And this is what Lucien did:

He designed ⅓ page ads for a few trade publications that were demonstrations in print—the ads said: "Dumps Itself, Rights Itself, Pays for Itself." They were couponed. He got Mr. Roura to agree to answer the best sounding inquiries by long distance telephone and try to send a trial hopper. He designed direct mail follow-up for the marginal inquiries and for those prospects who were only lukewarm on the phone. As soon as a few sales were made in prestige companies he got case histories which said much the same thing, but put the story on the premises of a satisfied user. Then he persuaded Roura to start case history publicity in trade magazines. A small, rather routine communications job.

The Roura ads are still ⅓ pages. The budget is still less than $50,000. But the Roura company is much, much larger. New jobs have been created. The product builds its own repeat sales. The price has held the line. A useful, strong, happy business has been established and free enterprise is the better for it.

This is Lucien's proudest accomplishment, though he has created many high-priced, four-color campaigns.

And this is one of the reasons we still don't have a minimum size for accounts. We have only minimum size for aspirations.

We've done something we are proud of, and you can't take it away from us, and you can't tear down anyone who helped do it.

121

I wish we had a hundred stories like this! We want very badly to have them, one day. We've never made much money from the Roura account (though we've never lost a cent on it, and they didn't want us to), but these kinds of successes aren't measured in immediate dollars. They are measured in pride and satisfaction that will spread to all accounts. Little pebbles make big waves. They will drive business to us, because clients can be led to want excellence to the same degree that we want it ourselves.

We are humble, believe me. We are also idealistic, but I hope not unrealistic. We have made only tiny, tentative strides along the way. But we do have a corporate conviction.

That conviction is that if 99 per cent of what we do today for our client falls somewhat short of excellence, we must try terribly hard tomorrow to cut it to zero per cent. And the next day I think we'll try again. We'll never make it, of course, but some days we may come awfully close.

Our foe is not dishonesty; it's laziness.

The men who will tear us down, if this ever happens, will not be in Cambridge or Washington; they will be on Madison Avenue or Michigan Avenue or Wilshire Boulevard or on streets that carry no symbolic name, but are just as much a part of advertising as Standard Rate and Data.

We're going to be trying very hard not to ruin your business for you.

I hope you'll try to return the favor.

MORE ON THE PURSUIT OF EXCELLENCE

(A Look at the Role of Advertising)

This noon here at 42nd Street and Lexington Avenue you have gathered for lunch somewhat left of center of the most extensive and expensive collection of advertising and public relations people in the world.

I strongly suspect that this is the first time your group has been left of center on anything, although you are forgiven, for your position is geographical rather than ideological.

Anyway, since the center of population of the New York advertising world is somewhere up about 50th and Madison, you are seated on the fringes of Mecca. For a half a buck cab fare, I'm sure you could get a thousand men willing and able to speak to you on the subtitle of my talk.

Regrettably, I can't.

Let me explain.

Someone on your program committee heard that I have been stumbling around the country with a speech titled "On the Pursuit of Excellence." I always use that title; it is full of both promise and ambiguity and like a *Better Homes & Gardens* decorating scheme, it fits all occasions.

At this point your promotion manager decided you wouldn't understand that title, which of course is the whole point in it, so your advance promotion gives me a subtitle: "A look at the role of advertising and how it assists the architect in the pursuit of architectural excellence."

If you parse that sentence quickly, it breaks into two parts. The first calls for an examination of the role of advertising.

I beg off. The water is too deep, the tide too swift, the shore too distant to take that on in a 20-minute swim after lunch. We'd both have stomach cramps, you and I. Some of our learned advertising associations are at this very time jabbing around among economists and business leaders looking for some expert testimony on this extremely complex subject.

Now as to how advertising assists the architect in the pursuit of architectural excellence—I'm sorry, but I guess I think it doesn't much. I have a hunch that exposing a poorly trained, or unimaginative or easy-going architect to superior advertising isn't going to have much effect. Conversely, I suspect that if all architectural advertising was

crummy, it wouldn't restrain the design and engineering brilliance of the finest architects very much. Which is not to say that good advertising fails if it is addressed to good architects.

I'd rather talk to you, these next few minutes, about the pursuit of excellence in any form, in your industry or mine, and about the costs of settling for less.

Everyone wants to excel. All God's Children, in one way or another, pay homage to the excellent.

The young student of architecture would like very much to become a Sullivan, Wright, Stone, Harrison or Abramovitz.

The young advertising writer dreams of being a Hopkins, Barton, Burnett, Young or Ogilvy.

The young lawyer dares to hope, at least for a little while, that he will become a Darrow, Holmes, Hand or Brandeis.

But, you say, these were men of extraordinary talent, and talent is not universal. It is found rarely, and is partly hereditary and isn't really fully understood.

It's a little easier to analyze excellence if we move away from the arts and professions.

Up on 53rd Street there is a restaurant operated by a man named Roger Chauveron. He founded and built the Chambord restaurant to its eminence; sold it to retire, got restless and started over again with the Chauveron, and made his second great success.

Through recipes? You could look up every dish at the cookbook counter in Brentano's or Doubleday's.

Through prices? The Chauveron, and the Chambord before it, charged as much as was necessary to make a profit on the finest food and service.

Through decor? The Chauveron, while extremely pleasant, is no showcase.

Through personal magnetism? Monsieur Chauveron, while courteous and hospitable, is no Toots Shor. When the house buys a drink the walls shake.

But—Monsieur Chauveron buys the best—always. Every day. Every item. Personally.

His restaurant is spotless. Every part of it. Dining room, kitchen, bar.

He roams constantly. He inspects food before it is served to you from the serving table. He will tell a waiter to change to a clean apron in mid-meal. He will rearrange the hors d'oeuvres cart five times a lunch period. He never stops. He never quits worrying.

And no great restaurant you ever visited was any different.

Let's go as far afield as possible for another illustration . . . the tired, discouraged, harassed railroad industry.

In the hollow pit of the depression, the General Motors Corporation performed one of the greatest feats of excellent salesmanship this country has ever known. It dieselized the American railroads, against their will, and if it had not the condition of the railroads today, bad as it is, would be infinitely worse.

Many of you know this relatively recent bit of business history. The Electro-Motive Division of GM set out to sell diesel engines as a replacement for the old steam locomotives. Doors were closed on the Electro-Motive salesmen despite demonstrations, engineering data, offers of trials and so on. The railroads understood the steam engine, they were used to it, and anyway most of them hauled a lot of coal. I have talked to some of those early salesmen and their success was hard work, attention to detail, imaginative presentation, over and over to the same people twenty, thirty, a hundred times. All the genius and engineering excellence that Boss Kettering put into the development of the engine paid off only when the same excellence was reached in the sales performance.

Today IBM is the undisputed leader in electronic data processing. Why? Because it was first in? Because it had vastly superior equipment? Because of lower prices?

None of these things is true. IBM was beaten into the data processing business by several other companies. The early publicity and the pioneer sales went to others while IBM hurried to catch up with its product. In many another

125

industry a company in the position of IBM would have fought a delaying action, pooh-poohing the new competitive equipment, or if not, being caught so far behind that it never caught up. That's what happened, for instance, to nearly every competitor General Motors had in the locomotive business.

But IBM isn't that kind of a company. From a late start, without getting into any kind of a price war, it caught up with and passed every competitor in sales and in total product.

It is easy to say IBM had more resources—more salesmen and more engineers, more customers, more money.

It is much more accurate to say that IBM had better trained and better motivated salesmen and engineers, more satisfied customers, and a better understanding of the constructive use of money.

It is easy to say of a man, or a company, or an industry, that it succeeded because of great talent, or fortuitous timing, or similar uncontrollable factors. This is a comfortable rationalization because it fits us all and forgives us equally. Unfortunately for our peace of mind, it just isn't true.

Rationalizing is like taking drugs. Responsibility for your own acts mists away. Rationalizing is always done sitting or lying down, never while walking hurriedly. Through some biological quirk, it is almost impossible to walk fast and at the same time feel sorry for yourself, or admit impotency, or accept a position of inferiority. The trick, then, is somehow to walk fast all the time. Satchel Paige says: "Never look back; something may be gaining on you."

It becomes progressively more difficult to keep moving, to maintain individuality, to cherish individual responsibility. You who are architects and we who are advertising men should understand better than most that excellence of any kind rests on skilled, trained, but most of all, highly motivated, individuals.

Perhaps, you who are architects are satisfied with the

plans for housing and business that are coming off the drawing boards at this point. I am not qualified to comment, but several recent personal experiences make me suspicious that architecture, like advertising, is falling victim of resignation to deadlines, dullness and defeat.

Jenkin Lloyd Jones, the editor of the *Tulsa Tribune,* who by the way is a nephew of Frank Lloyd Wright, made a wonderful speech to Midwestern newspaper editors last fall, and it has been widely reprinted, so some of you may have seen it. But for those who haven't, let me quote a few of his observations.

Jones is talking about our ideological struggle against the forces of communism. He says: "Do you know what scares me about the Communists? It is not their political system, which is primitive and savage. It is not their economic system, which works so badly that progress in a few directions is purchased at the price of progress in all the rest. It is their puritanism. It is their dedication and self sacrifice. It does no good to comfort ourselves with the reflection that these are the products of endless brainwashings, of incessant propaganda, of deprivation by censorship and jamming of counter-information and contrary arguments. The dedication is there. The confidence that they are morally superior is there.

"And what of us?

"Well . . . we are now at the end of the third decade of the national insanity known as 'progressive education.' This was the education where everybody passes, where the report cards were non-committal lest the failure be faced with the fact of his failure, where all moved at a snail's pace like a transatlantic convoy so that the slowest need not be left behind, and all proceeded toward adulthood in the lockstep of 'togetherness.' Thus, the competition that breeds excellence was to be sacrificed for something called 'life adjustment.'

"With what results? We have produced tens of thousands of high school graduates who move their lips as they read and cannot write a coherent paragraph."

127

And at the same time, as Mr. Jones points out, ". . . our Russian contemporaries, who were supposed to be dedicated to the mass man, have been busy constructing a scientific, professional and educational elite, while we have been engaged in the wholesale production of mediocrity."

A few weeks ago I was in Germany on business for the second time in a couple of years. What I see there worries me; not militarily—I think the Germans want war even less than we do if that is possible. But I think we have cause for economic worry. Postwar Germany has developed remarkably high standards of personal responsibility. Competition is so intense that the gifted have to work awfully hard and awfully well to excel. In this climate—where secretaries work from 8 A.M. to 6 P.M. and where managers work longer by a couple of hours—a whole country is being rebuilt both physically and spiritually while we let our people come in at 10 o'clock and shrug it off as the fault of the New Haven Railroad.

Relief is becoming an honorable career in America. Nothing is your fault.

We had a stenographer in our New York office a couple of years ago who quit, at the same time her husband quit his job, and they both went to California for six months' vacation. New York mailed their unemployment checks to them. Without too much trouble, they got by in a beach house on $84.00 a week net. When the payments ran out, they came back to New York and we were nuts enough to hire her back. She soon began coming in late all the time. She was warned a dozen times and finally we fired her. She applied for unemployment compensation again, only this time we objected. After a hearing and an appeal we finally kept her from collecting unemployment and she had to get a job.

Alas, however, the welfare state is rigged for the lazy and the cheat. She worked three or four weeks somewhere else, got fired and applied for unemployment again. Under our nutty laws, since her last employer didn't file against her, she was on the rolls again. But since she worked for

128

him only a couple of weeks, only a couple of weeks of her compensation was charged against his account and the rest was charged against us, since we were her employer of longer record. And we couldn't do anything about it because we weren't her last employer despite the fact that two different state examiners had found that she had been fired for good cause.

Well, I've been ranting on about what is wrong and I'd like to talk just a few more minutes about what I think we can do about it. I can best do this by telling you what our firm is trying to do to get back to a hardheaded pursuit of excellence.

In the unemployment case I mentioned just now, there is one small clue. We fight every claim for unemployment if it isn't justified. If someone quit to loaf, if someone got fired because they wouldn't work, we give them fits in the unemployment channels. It's so easy to say that since only part of the claim gets charged to you, it's cheaper to let it go. But I'll tell you since we got tough about this we've had less turnover and that's money right into our profit-sharing plan.

We don't let people drift in at whatever time they want. This starts with management, and includes everyone. We say if you can't depend on the New Haven, we can't depend on you. One of us has to make new arrangements.

We are very hot for clean desks. That's no easier to enforce in an advertising agency than an architect's office, but it can be done. Messy desks and messy minds and messy advertising are to some degree related.

We are trying to hire the best people we possibly can—all businesses do that—but more important we are working very hard to try to eliminate from our staffs those of low ambition or limited ability.

These are only a few of the things that we can do—and you can do—to restore the pursuit of excellence to a corporate way of life.

In the long run, people will rebel against mediocrity or cheapness. To compare discount houses with human re-

sponsibility may be stretching for an analogy and yet I think there is an easily understood lesson here.

One of the first discount houses in America was Sol Polk's in Chicago. In the early wave of discounters Polk screamed out its prices, but it became great only when it set up one of the finest appliance servicing organizations in the country.

Plain pipe racks have no lasting appeal to anyone—in merchandising, in advertising, in architecture. Korvette has moved to Fifth Avenue. Orbach's advertises style. Volkswagen, an inexpensive car, trumpets its quality, and Lincoln Center goes to Max Abramovitz to design a great Philharmonic Hall.

We are that rarity among advertising agencies—an advertiser. It is significant, I think, that among all the advertisements we have run in our own behalf that an ad from our *Wall Street Journal* campaign was the best read we have ever prepared. Over 25,000 reprints have been distributed, 225 of them, by the way, being sent out by one of the leading architectural firms in the country. It is headed "Why Leaders Win Price Wars," and I'd like to read you just a couple of paragraphs:

"Part of being a leader is being able to withstand the arrows of price competition. A leader need not be the biggest or the oldest company in its field, but it's the one that stands out because it is recognized as the best. It wins price wars because its reputation for excellence in its field will not be obliterated by price-cutting.

"A leader is also usually a living—and very healthy—testimonial to the effectiveness of an important marketing principle:

"That in the long run it profits you far more to sell your product on its *value* rather than on its *price*.

"Almost everyone will agree with that principle in theory; but many violate it in practice. It is often so easy to pick up quick sales by promoting 'special prices' or 'deals.' And it is so hard to resist the temptation to fight fire with fire when price-cutting competitors are apparently hurting you.

130

"Perhaps the main reason more manufacturers do not sell on value rather than on price is that selling on value is far more difficult than selling on price. It requires, of course, a product that *has* value. But that is only the beginning.

"It also requires the marketing wisdom to know what specific 'character' you should create for your product to separate it most favorably from all others of its kind. Then it requires the creative skill to crystallize that character on paper or on the air waves, and project it into the minds of the right people at the right time . . .

"It requires something else, too—the lonely courage to stand out from the crowd, to *tell your own story consistently,* year in and year out, regardless of the opportunistic tactics of competition. Perhaps this is the rarest quality of all. It is sometimes called Leadership."

And that, I think, is the remedy for fast, fast, fast relief from mediocrity in all its manifestations.

You and I have this opportunity for leadership. We have the opportunity to insist on quality in our advertising, in our architecture, in what we buy and what we do and who we hire and who we fire and what principles we accept and what we reject.

The man who has discovered the rewards of excellence; the man who has come to cringe before mediocrity knows deep in his heart when he has succeeded and when he has failed.

International Marketing and Advertising

For many years, there have been a few U. S. agencies operating around the world. It was not, however, until the late 1950s and the early 1960s that the real expansion of American marketing and advertising took place overseas.

Although Marsteller Inc. was by no means one of the first U. S. agencies to establish its own offices in Europe, it was probably one of the smallest to invest a substantial portion of its assets overseas. This was through no foresight or conviction on Bill Marsteller's part. He made his first trip to Europe in 1959 with two associates, in his words "kicking and screaming every inch of the way."

However, he quickly became convinced that there were great opportunities abroad and, shedding his midwestern isolationist background, plunged into the development of an international business without reserve.

One outcome was a widely reprinted speech he made at the opening of a two-week meeting of several hundred international agency executives from around the world. The meeting proceeded from New York to Washington to White Sulphur Springs to Chicago, and the talk, reprinted here, is an attempt to explain the kind of American marketing man these advertising leaders, many of whom had never been in the U. S. before, would be likely to encounter.

THE NEW AMERICAN MARKETING MAN

There is nothing new in American business enterprises becoming deeply involved in world markets. Coca-Cola is everywhere. The IBM salesman speaks a hundred tongues. Procter & Gamble washes silk saris and dacron dresses. J. Walter Thompson and McCann-Erickson are familiar names in cities many Americans scarcely know exist.

Yet the biggest continuing news story in the business press and in marketing and advertising trade publications has been the emergence of the American as an international businessman.

What has happened, of course, is that world trade is no longer the business of the few but of the many. A natural result is the appearance of a new American marketing man —a man somewhat different from the limited number of world-oriented Americans who have been at this thing a long time. Let me illustrate.

A few weeks ago I talked to the President of a substantial manufacturing concern in Indiana. He was just back from his second trip to Europe. In September he will make his first trip to the Philippines, Australia and Japan. He is 53 years old and has been President of his Company for six years. His Company has sales of about $125,000,000, is No. 1 in its field, and has grown steadily since 1947 with reasonable profits every year.

In 1950, 94 per cent of its sales were domestic and 6

135

per cent were export. There were no licensees or overseas manufacturing plants.

By contrast, in 1960, 81 per cent of sales were domestic, 3 per cent were export, and 14 per cent were from a joint-venture company and licensee.

By 1965, his total sales were up another 50 per cent. By this time he had little or no export sales, but approximately a third of his total sales will come from two joint-venture companies and one wholly-owned foreign subsidiary.

He should be a happy man, comfortable with his progress in changing his Company from an American marketer to a world marketer. But he is ill at ease, frustrated, and feeling a little insecure. He's been having some new experiences.

He speaks no language other than English. When he was preparing for his first trip to Europe, his friends told him, "Don't worry about it; everyone in Europe speaks English." And mostly they did. But when he got to his joint-venture company in West Germany, he found that superintendents and foremen didn't—or they did so with great difficulty— and he wanted badly to compliment them on their work; to show them that he respected what they had accomplished. Through an interpreter he realized that the words were coming through but that his conviction and esteem were not. The personality that is so warm and winning in Indiana was simply neutral in Germany.

In France, he met with a licensee and two attorneys to agree on a contract modification. Sales compensation was stated in New Francs in the document, and he found that he was the only one who could not quickly and mentally relate dollars and francs. In his pocket he had a plastic currency converter, but he was too embarrassed to use it.

In Belgium, a business associate had a dinner party for him, and the conversation kept getting back into French and losing him. He found himself realizing that there was really something faintly insulting in the whole situation: they were vaguely irritated that here was another American businessman, anxious to be a part of their economy, but

136

unwilling to be a part of their culture; he was remotely annoyed because here was a group of people, anxious to make or sell his products, who couldn't understand what he believed to be the universal language of business.

And so my friend is a little unhappy about the One-Worldness his Company is so rapidly embracing.

I have deep sympathy for him. I've had every one of those experiences myself. He and I are statistical norms— we are case histories of the average of the New American Marketing Man.

Let me tell you a little bit about this American marketing man with whom so many of you will deal increasingly in the years just ahead.

I have the names of just over 100 United States companies which in the last ten years have moved firmly into international marketing through new establishments which they own or operate, through joint ventures, or through strong minority positions in existing companies elsewhere.

First a word about the companies themselves—they are smaller than you might think. Most of them have sales of less than $50,000,000. The fields in which they operate rank in this order, in terms of number of companies: chemicals, machinery, food, electrical machinery and transportation equipment. A large number of them, therefore, are in industrial, rather than consumer, marketing. They have no large, mature, experienced international management staff.

Now let's look at the men who run these new international marketing activities. I have tried to collect some data on the chief executives and the chief marketing executives, where available, from the various editions of "Who's Who" —national, regional or industry editions.

By far the largest number of them are in the age bracket of 47 to 55. They were born during or just after World War I; therefore, their schooling and their formative years were in the backwash of that war. They started their business careers, for the most part, during the great depression. While many were in military service in World War II, con-

137

siderably fewer than half of them, it appears, had service overseas.

It will come as a shock, perhaps, that relatively few of them grew up in the cosmopolitan centers of the East—the areas around New York, Boston and Washington, for instance. It seems the substantial majority were born in the Middle West and educated solely in public schools (not to be confused with the British definition of public schools). A few others came from the Southwest, but only the West was the environmental base for fewer of them than the Northeast.

Of those who now live in our larger and more cosmopolitan cities (and a good many still do not), where contact with non-Americans is commonplace, most of them were fully grown and had business experience behind them when they got there.

I am sure that my friends in statistical research would find little value in the summary I have just given you, but I believe it is a composite of sociological factors which strongly influence why those of us who somewhat suddenly find ourselves in a whole new framework of marketing experiences sometimes react as we do.

Like human beings everywhere, the American business and marketing executive is the product of his environment to a marked degree. He was shaped by the part of the country he came from, the kind of education he had, the ideologies of his parents, friends and teachers, the editorial position of the newspaper to which he was exposed, the current of the times in which he got his first conscious assimilation of basic principles.

The summary I gave you earlier is a capsule of his environment. Forgive me, please, if I sometimes use myself as a case in point, but I am almost exactly this norm or average.

We grew up, as I have said, in the wake of World War I. This was not a time, in America, when our love of the rest of the world was great. The teaching of German was forbidden by law in many schools. I was bitterly ashamed of

the fact that my grandparents were born in Germany and sometimes conversed with my mother in German; I shut my ears to it, anxious to learn none of it, and succeeded wonderfully.

The Mayor of Chicago ordered textbooks burned that treated the American Revolution in such a way as to report the British position without prejudice or passion.

Only little Finland seemed disposed to pay its war debts. The rest of the world, so it seemed to us then, was at best irresponsible, at worst, dishonest.

Except for the handful of today's business executives who grew up in a city like New York, we never saw a French menu, heard an Italian opera, or ate off Irish linen. If we heard another language spoken, it was by recent immigrants, who were sensitive about their backgrounds, and were almost always in the common labor or domestic servant classifications.

At church and Sunday school, we were encouraged to give to "foreign" missions in order to bring light to "heathens." "Alien" property sounded like it had been stolen. Words like "foreign," "alien," "immigrant," and "heathen" all blended together with an unpleasant connotation. We even had a popular song about the "heathen" Chinese.

What encouragement was there, under these circumstances, to learn another language? Perhaps I'm an extreme case, but I got through a first-class grammar and high school and graduated from one of the best and largest universities in the United States with no language training, other than English, except for two very dispirited years of instruction in textbook Latin.

Then we went out to work in a country in which there were vast numbers of unemployed. No one was quite sure what had happened to our wonderful, self-sufficient economy, but one very popular villain was foreign imports. Our business was being undersold by foreign competition; our tariff barriers, many thought, were simply not high enough in view of the ridiculously low labor rates throughout the world.

We became junior executives in a political climate which was frankly experimental and anti-business. Some of us had our first experience with labor unions and found that all too often, in their formative years, they were communist-influenced, or at least patterned after the organizational tactics of labor movements in other countries. The mushrooming labor unions of the 1930's openly appealed to the more newly arrived of our citizens who were the least favored members of our work force. We found ourselves negotiating labor contracts with muscular men who often had weak education and foreign accents. We didn't much like it.

If we exported products, we had trouble getting our money because of currency regulations or simple inability to pay.

Many of us had personal experience with outright expropriation of our trademarks or our product designs, and we didn't know how to protect ourselves.

And so these or similar factors developed a strong core of isolationist thinking in business management.

Now the years have gone by, and a dramatic and difficult thing has happened to us.

High-speed transportation, modern communication devices, another World War, a new kind of freedom in many other countries, tightening competition and coming market saturation at home—these and other things have forced us to reconsider our basic beliefs and, perhaps, prejudices.

The final blow, of course, was the coming of the European Common Market.

For many of us it has been a painful transition to realize that isolationism is no longer practical, assuming it once was.

You'll have to be a little patient with us. Many of us are finding it is much more difficult to learn a second language than it is for our children, who are now being exposed to a second, third or fourth language as routinely as are children in schools in other parts of the world.

This is in spite of the fact that one of the most dynamic

businesses in America today is the Berlitz language schools which are jammed with businessmen trying desperately to fill in the gaps in their education.

We still have a great deal to learn about world trade—perhaps not Coca-Cola, or IBM, or Procter & Gamble, or the like, who were farsighted enough long enough ago, to see what would happen—but most of us who are smaller or less sophisticated.

Yet, if we didn't have something to offer you, there would be no reason for you to work with us in all these promising new joint ventures and cross-licensing arrangements.

In some cases it is obviously dollars that motivate you. But clearly this is an insecure and temporary platform for a business partnership. Something more must come from us if you are to welcome us into your economies as the associates or competitors of your own businesses.

First, I expect, we must face the reality of welcoming you into *our* economy. It is interesting, I think, that as our own rather small agency has been establishing itself in the international field, fully half the agencies we have talked with abroad have been as much interested in what we could do for them in the United States as they have been in how we might work with them in their own country.

Second, I think we must unlock not only our files and records, but our hearts and minds, and give you full access to whatever we may have learned about marketing—about advertising, public relations, selling. I think that while your manufacturing techniques in many cases have caught up with us, and in some cases passed us, that only the most nationalistic of our friends from abroad will deny that we have been experimenting longer and more broadly in communications and selling.

Such knowledge as we have must be shared with you; but not imposed upon you. It will have to be taken in bits and pieces and fitted to local conditions, national traditions, professional codes of conduct, and cultural climates.

The new American marketing man is changing quite a

bit. He may still order bourbon and soda instead of wine, simply because he likes it better, but he is much less likely than formerly to run an advertisement in Brussels that hasn't been prepared by citizens of Belgium.

He may still want to buy a share of an agency in London, but he is much more likely to be willing—even anxious—to exchange shares in an agency in New York.

He may still wonder if he dares commit his stockholders' money to joint or sole development of business in those of the Latin American countries where there has been political instability, but he can no longer simply comfortably turn his back to the problem.

He may be unable to identify the three largest cities in India, but he will be able to name the three most progressive advertising agencies—or valve manufacturing firms, for that matter.

Most of all, he's coming to like and respect his business associates in other countries. He's less critical of the way business is done outside the United States.

Of course, there are some things he still doesn't understand and can't help being just a little impatient about.

Because he is dedicated to running his business on facts, he worries about investing money in new plants and new products when the data on the market potential are so thin. He gags a bit at placing advertising in publications without independent circulation audits. He'd like to know a great deal more about how individual customers and prospects in your country really live. He'd like a lot better evidence on how your business enterprises buy, and what they buy, and what they won't buy. And just your word isn't enough. It isn't that he doesn't trust you—he has learned not to always trust even his own judgment.

Mostly, though, he's a good man. Takes a bit of understanding, but he'll become a profitable, pleasant and dependable ally.

If we—you and I—can make even half of these hundreds of new international business partnerships work out, men and women throughout the world will be the beneficiaries.

Obviously they will benefit from new opportunities to share in the world's products. But most of all, through understanding we will have done more for peace than can ever be negotiated at a political conference table.

Advertising Principles

A subject that has interested advertisers and agencies as well as the business community generally is the role and compensation of the advertising agency. Two speeches, "Can Fees Replace Media Commissions?" and "The Advertising Agency—Whose Agent?" are addressed to these relationships. The first was a speech before an American Association of Advertising Agencies convention and the second a speech before advertisers and agencies in several locations.

Two other typical statements of advertising principles are an article in the magazine *Sales Management,* "How to Get the Most Out of Your Ad Agency" and "Must the Calendar Rule Advertising?", which appeared in the old *Printers Ink* and was reproduced by a number of publishers for dissemination to the advertising customers.

CAN FEES REPLACE MEDIA COMMISSIONS?

This talk started in New York last January on a very snowy morning.

We were conducting weekly training seminars for a half-dozen new and young account and creative men and the leader scheduled for that particular morning commutes by the New Haven railroad and I filled in for him. The subject was to be our charging methods—how time charges are computed, which out-of-pocket costs are and are not marked up, and so on.

We never got very far into those specifics because it was so quickly apparent that our young people knew very little about the underlying philosophies of agency compensation, and almost nothing about the history of the agency business.

Most of them have come into the business at a time when the trade press has been full of many stories on the desirability of fees as a method of payment for advertising agency service; when the principle of media paying a commission to advertising agencies has been under question again, as it has periodically for over fifty years. Most of them have read that agency commissions are illogical at best, and at worst perhaps even unethical, without ever knowing how agency commissions came into being, why they have continued as the primary source of advertising agency income, or without ever truly examining what effect different kinds of compensation have upon both the effectiveness and the cost of advertising.

147

I am fairly sure our people are not uniquely ignorant in this area. At least some of your ex-employees who have offered to solve our management problems for us don't seem to be much more lettered in the history and theory of compensation than our own people.

I don't know what, if anything, you feel it is desirable to tell your people about agency compensation, but let me tell you what we tell our people.

First of all, we say there is no such thing as standardized agency compensation. For instance, just about 50 per cent of our income comes from fees while for some agencies it will be perhaps 80 or 85 per cent commissions and 10 to 15 per cent fees. This is because, first of all, agencies differ in the kind of business they attract and the kind of services they provide. For instance, we are deeply involved in public relations and direct mail and collateral and similar non-commissionable activities; other agencies may choose to specialize in media advertising. Then, too, there is a difference in kind of accounts.

Then we point out that although there has been talk about fee compensation for years, A.A.A.A. figures show no appreciable gain in the use of fees as a substitute for commissions as a basic foundation of agency compensation. To understand why, we say, you need to look into how agency commissions came about at all.

Nearly all advertising people know that the agency business started as a quite different structure. The early advertising agents were not agents at all, but space brokers. They made deals with publishers for space at a price and sold it for what they could get for it and the difference was the broker's profit. A few of them, to gain a competitive advantage, began to prepare advertising or to make copy recommendations to advertisers. It was their success in increasing the use of advertising, compared to the straight broker, that led to the development of the real forerunner of the advertising agency of today.

At just about the turn of the century, a group of magazine publishers called the Quoin Club concluded that those

space brokers who were really performing a service for the advertiser were at the same time performing a service for the media which justified compensation from the media. The publishers said, in effect, "If you will help develop advertising that will make my publication a more successful medium, instead of simply buying and selling space, we will pay you a commission for this extra service."

This is how it started, but by no means did all media embrace this theory at once. In fact, we point out, it was a gradual acceptance that took 35 years and a few of us started in this business in time to see some of it happen.

I, for instance, can remember when one of the large magazine publishing houses granted no agency commission. Since there was no cost advantage to the advertisers, most of their space was placed directly. As a substitute for agencies, the publisher maintained an "advertising service department" which, on order of the space salesman, prepared speculative ads. The space salesman took them out to the advertisers and tried to sell, first of all, the copy and layout, and secondly, his publication.

Well, the problems are evident. The copy and layout weren't very closely associated with the advertiser's sales plan. The copy was often written simply from a catalog, or a space salesman's call report. The same writer often wrote ads for competitive companies on the same day for the same issue of the same magazine.

On the other hand, those publications which had disbanded their service departments and had encouraged advertising agencies to develop the actual advertisements were getting better looking ads and growing faster. They had let competition between agencies raise advertising creative standards, while reserving to themselves competition on the merits of their circulation and editorial.

Lest you think this is all ancient history you can find advertising service departments with paste-pots and shears in hundreds of daily newspapers, busily turning out retail ads from mat books because the compensation structure of the daily newspaper has not encouraged the development of

149

strong, imaginative local agencies in any number. The downstate Illinois newspaper where I got my first job still, first of all, sells ads, and only then sells advertising. My father was a neighborhood grocer in that town when the chain store revolution took place and he was forced to the wall not so much by lower prices as by being out-advertised, out-merchandized, out-displayed, out-promoted generally, and the only consultant available to him was a Meyer Both mat book.

So you see, agencies do perform a service for the media. We've talked only about the creative service, because that is the one most often overlooked and is the one most difficult to transplant to the media—or, for that matter, to the client. But we do other things, of course—and at this point we suggest our people read Fred Gamble's fine discussion "What Advertising Agencies Are—What They Do and How They Do It."

In summing up on that media-advertising agency relationship we like to go back to a statement by Frank Braucher, back in 1941, on behalf of the Magazine Publishers Association. He said:

"There are certainly many agents who do not understand the publishers' theory of the agency commission. Simply stated it is this: *the publisher pays a commission to the agent for services rendered to the advertiser.* Various attempts have been made to get something different out of it, but the fact still remains, I repeat, that the publishers pay a commission to the agent for services rendered to the advertiser."

It isn't surprising that many of our people don't understand what it is that the media get in return for the commission they pay the advertising agency; even many teachers of advertising don't. And certainly many businessmen don't.

Next we point out to our people that advertisers can buy direct from a medium if they choose to do so. But if a medium believes that advertising agency health is essential to

the economics of its business, if it believes agencies perform a service in keeping with what it pays them, then there is a reason for it to allow commissions to agencies.

In fact, this is common throughout American industry. A grocery wholesaler buys a case of Post Toasties and gets a discount because he is performing warehousing and distribution services. An architect or decorator gets a discount for providing design and coordinating services. A manufacturer often gets a discount for O. E. M. purchases because he may be faced with the ultimate problems of field service.

Pricing advertising service is a very difficult and arbitrary business. Like pricing any other business compounded of talent and invention and risk and experience. Like pricing an operation for a spinal fusion. Like pricing an acquittal—or a conviction. Like pricing an oil painting. Hours expended, or materials and labor, or cost plus—all of these have at least as many abuses as do commissions.

But the price for advertising service, we keep pointing out, is indeed subject to negotiation. Some services we perform for clients produce no commission income because they are services only for the client and not for a medium, so we negotiate compensation from the client. And sometimes—in our kind of an agency quite often—we put in so much time on a client's advertising or marketing plans and the execution of them that even though the result is largely commissionable space, the commission simply is inadequate to meet our costs. Whenever this is the case, we must negotiate further income.

But you see, what fees a client pays us does not change the fact that media pay us a commission for doing something for them they would otherwise have to do themselves and pay for in other ways—creative service departments, increased production and traffic staffs (since advertising would come from so many more sources), increased billing staffs (since the number of transactions for the same sales volume would be greatly increased), and so on.

151

In fact, we say to our young people, if media commissions were eliminated entirely it is highly unlikely that media costs would be reduced at all.

Then we point out that the advertising agency structure is the very antithesis of monopoly. One of the most important factors in producing good advertising has been that the agency is constantly aware of the fact that if it does not do a good job there is another agency just around the corner willing to come in and take over.

While it is not directly related to the principle of agency commissions, whether clients could over a very long period produce as good advertising is in our mind doubtful. In the advertiser company, advertising is simply one of the functions involved in conducting the business, but in the advertising agency it is the end product. In the client company, making better advertising may get a share of management attention, but there are the proper diversions of management into manufacturing, product research, industrial relations, plant expansion, patents, purchasing, cost controls and dozens of other things only vaguely, if at all, related to advertising. However, in the agency, management attention is focused continuously on advertising and its directly related functions. Agency management is advertising management. In an advertising agency the president is virtually always an advertising man. This single-minded concentration on one of the functions of the business is the greatest asset of the independent agency, in my opinion, and is something we must learn to explain to those who are not in the agency business, who have not lived in the climate where the creation of advertising permeates the whole enterprise.

I said the advertising agency is the antithesis of monopoly and I think it can be demonstrated by illustrating another service the agency performs for media—that of creating new advertisers and thereby creating new competition in the marketplace.

Our agency, like the vast majority of agencies, started with small accounts. Many of our clients didn't even have an advertising manager, and the president or sales manager

or someone else tried to do what little he could to make the company and its products known. We came into the picture in most cases because a media salesman had uncovered the manufacturer as a prospect, but either the ads offered the publisher or broadcaster were so primitive that the media hesitated to take them, or there was simply no one else to do the preparation. In this way new agencies are made—by working with media to make new advertisers.

I give you just one case in point. The Roura Iron Works of Detroit, Mich., was one of our early clients and still is. From a non-advertiser it has become a regular user of a dozen publications in less than ten years and the company has become an aggressive competitor in the materials handling field. We have done advertising, both publication and direct mail, publicity, and market research for them on an integrated basis. They have had part-time service from a dozen experienced specialists only because a space salesman had the incentive to send them to us to help develop and execute their advertising plan to the mutual interest of client, agency and media.

There is another great strength in the decision of media to allow commissions to agencies. It lies in the relationship created between media and agencies.

If there were no media commissions, there would be little reason for media salesmen and publishers to work with agencies. If the buying decision seems to be solely that of the client, if the order comes from him, if the bill goes to him, why should media come to us except as an occasional courtesy?

When you say this to some of the young people, they say, "Wouldn't that be great—no more time wasted with media people!" And that attitude, which seems to be growing among your people and mine, is one of the real hidden threats to the successful conduct of a strong advertising agency business.

The function of an advertising agency as it has evolved, I need hardly remind you, is not simply to make layouts and write copy and film commercials. It is, for the client, to

select from among the powerful communications forces available those which are most appropriate for him, and then to execute his sales message in the brightest and most compelling way appropriate to the medium.

I am deeply disturbed that so many advertising agency people are being bred to look upon media representatives as a nuisance. I am concerned that so many media people believe that agency media buying is often superficial and conducted at arm's length from the account and creative people with the responsibility to put the plan into effect.

Our best communications plans, our most creative advertising, surely need all the market information we can assimilate, and traditionally the first best source has been the medium of the market. If we are finding media less helpful today, I suspect most of the fault is our own. If we find the new media salesmen coming into the business today less able to help us make maximum effect with their medium, I expect much of the fault is our own.

Study after study—in Detroit, Chicago, New York and elsewhere—has shown that media complain about inability to see agency decision makers, about buyers who are inadequately trained in both their own function and the client's products and plans, about agency concern with pure quantitative measures, about unreasonable agency requests for uncompensated field studies, and, most of all, about simple rudeness and bad manners among agency people.

Even allowing for 50 per cent exaggeration, there must be an element of truth because the complaints are alarmingly universal. As the years go by, if this disaffection spreads, like any human or business relationship it can only end in some kind of separation or divorce.

As the advertising business has grown, I suspect there is less communication between the leaders of advertising agencies and the leaders of media. Even a relatively small agency today is bigger than many agencies considered quite large 25 years ago. We have therefore necessarily had to pass down many responsibilities once handled by top management. One of them is media relations. The publishers and

154

radio and TV are in much the same situation. It is increasingly difficult for them to maintain direct and frequent relations with all the agencies now placing important quantities
of business with them. I'm afraid all of us know a little less
each year about the true state of our media relations.

But I am convinced that none of these activities really
gets at the heart of strong media relations. The real core
is an understanding of what our relations with media *are*—
with the understanding that while we are indeed the agency
of the client, we are performing specific services for media
for which we are compensated by them.

It is time, I think, for each agency to reassess its attitude
toward media, and the attitude of its people toward media.
It is time to take inventory of what our people really know
about how we get paid and why. It is time to be sure that
their acts are not weakening the very relationship on which
at least a part of our compensation is based.

It is in this media-agency relationship that the answer to
the question of whether fees can replace agency commissions is to be found. As one of the managers of an agency
that gets barely half its income from commissions, perhaps
I should not be concerned. Surely we, as much as any
agency, would find a good future if we charged only fees.
But if we did I am convinced we would lose one of the
strongest ingredients in the building of successful advertising and that is the deep involvement of the media in which
it will ultimately appear.

In these days when the advertiser pressures to prove out
advertising effectiveness are increasing, those of us who are
involved in the creation and dissemination of advertising
messages should be increasing our inter-relationships. We
who are full time in the advertising business must be working together more closely on all things which will help us
make advertising more productive for the advertiser, whose
full-time business is something else entirely. And we should
be slow to discredit, I should think, a principle that has
helped bring the agency and the media together to build
advertising into the business power it is today.

155

THE ADVERTISING AGENCY—WHOSE AGENT?

There are a lot of ways I could rationalize the acceptance of this invitation tonight, but the truth is you are in our trade zone and one of my specifically assigned corporate responsibilities is new business.

So God love you, and thank you for asking me.

Those of you who work for agencies or media I didn't come particularly to see, but some of you are old friends and I hope all others will be new friends and we should be. We are drawn together by our common cause, which is to live off the advertiser.

I say this seriously, gratefully, and I hope, constructively. If you work for an agency or a medium or a supplier you share with me the reason for our economic existence—to make advertising a powerful force for profits. It has no other real purpose, and that in my opinion is something for which we should be glad, not apologetic.

The original invitation I got from you included this paragraph:

"We'd like you to come to Hartford and help us clear the air. Tell us about the problems of an agency—advertising's middleman. Tell us your gripes about client practices, publication practices, profit problems. Tell us how agency-client-media relationships can be improved to the benefit of all—and the profession of advertising."

Well, I'm not an expert on air pollution, but I will circle the rest of this meaty paragraph a few times until I'm out of wind or you're out of patience.

First, I'd like to underline a point of view I've already made—that it is the advertiser who is the key to the client-agency-media relationship.

Without advertisers there won't be any agencies and that would be the biggest possible problem an agency could have. Without advertisers there still would be trade and

156

technical publications, but they'd be far fewer and thinner and they wouldn't mean anything to the media people in this audience because you'd be selling lace instead of space.

I happen to be one of those who thinks that a lot of the troubles of that great debating society, the Association of Industrial Advertisers, comes from a lack of understanding of the relationships and purposes of the different ethnic groups in the club. I speak as a veteran and wearer of the Purple Heart.

I wasn't long a member of what was then called NIAA until I was part of a junta to overthrow the government, not because it was brutal, venal or corrupt, but because we thought it was aimless and confused. Our coup succeeded and eventually I wound up a part of the "in" group, and the tables were turned and now *we* were trying to put down the annual revolution by beaning the pickets with their own signs.

I believed then as an advertising manager, and I believe now as an agency man, that AIA should be run by and run for the advertiser. The test is this: if all the advertisers drop out, how many agency and media people do you think will patronize these barbecues?

This is not a speech about AIA. I put that speech into early retirement nearly 20 years ago when it became evident that it was impotent either to beget young or to comfort the aged.

The point, of course, is a reiteration that the advertiser is the key to the client-agency-media relationship.

Yet each party of this troika has certain unilateral motivations and rights.

The client's primary advertising aim is to sell his goods profitably. The medium's primary motive is to serve its reader, and all it sells advertisers is a share of an audience, real or alleged. The agency, however, is actually in business to serve the advertiser through the efficient preparation of promotion and advertising, while at the same time serving the medium by so doing.

157

I said that clients, agencies and media have some motivations and rights that are unique to each.

Among the rights the advertiser has are these:

1. The right to advertise or not, and where and when it wishes, and all an agency can do is advise, and then act by consent.
2. The right to use an agency or not, and for as much or as little of its promotion job as it wishes.
3. The right to hire and fire agencies, and to decide the conditions of their employment, including compensation.
4. The right to tell an agency as much or as little as it chooses about its business.

Among the rights individual media have are these:

1. To determine whether agencies—or which agencies—provide them with a useful service and to set their compensation for that service.
2. The right either to deal direct or through a channel of distribution common in the industry.
3. And most importantly, of course, to determine whether they wish to carry advertising at all or not, and what kind, and to set acceptance or rejection standards.

Among the rights of individual agencies are these:

1. The right to solicit and accept clients or to terminate their relationship, including the right to accept or reject conditions of employment.
2. The right to recommend for or against any medium or any type of media, and to establish conditions that insure its objectivity and freedom of choice.
3. The right to determine what parts of the client's promotion program it wishes to solicit.
4. The right to set the ground rules it believes necessary to fulfill its obligations to the client, or, failing this, to decline to serve the client.

Somehow I have a feeling that if we all thought a little harder about these obligations and rights and about our interrelationships there would be fewer association meetings given over to flagellation of one another. When I hear agency men air their gripes about clients, when I see media salesmen gather wood for agency witch-burning, when I hear advertising and sales promotion managers knocking together fences to protect themselves from media and agency people, I sadly recall a story.

It is about the cannibal who took another cannibal home to dinner. After they had eaten all they could the guest said, "You know, your wife certainly makes a wonderful stew, but don't you think you'll sort of miss her?"

So much for love-making; now let's get specific.

And that's the way it has to be—specific. In the final analysis, the only relationship that has any meaning is that between Client A and Agency B, or Agency C and Medium D, or Medium E and Client F and so on.

There are some media reps I wouldn't tell my middle name to because by morning it would be all over town misspelled into a dirty word. There are some clients we shouldn't work for because they wouldn't trust us, no matter what we recommended or how we got paid, and some clients we shouldn't work for because we don't know enough about their business *to be* trusted. At least one client ceased to respect us because we made a mistake on a couple of people on his account, and at least one client lost our respect because *he* made an uncorrected personnel mistake, too.

So it gets pretty individual, this relationship.

Back in the middle forties, one of the reasons I joined the radicals intent on overthrowing the NIAA Diet of Worms was because the Association had used up most of the national dues (which were then considered to be somewhat excessive at $5 annually) to make a movie which set out to prove that the industrial advertising manager is one hell of a guy, professional and all that. It also set out to prove that business papers were better than ever, and that

159

agencies were largely peopled by men who were as immaculately conceived as the founders of the Harvard Graduate School of Business.

Of course, in a few cases some ad managers, some media, some agency people were almost that good.

Those were the ones that never let their managements, their customers or their clients within 50 miles of the movie, which I recall as being 16 mm. in width, but only 8 mm. deep.

But the woolly heads among us cranked up their projectors and took to the hustings and our business was set back a decade in whatever is meant by professional standing.

You see, if the ad manager seemed weak and insecure to his management before the lights went out and the camera rolled, he looked pretty much the same, only more blurred, when the lights came on again. When an agency took it out to a client and it was over, the client looked and saw the same agency he saw before. And that's the way it will always be.

There were some specific questions posed in the announcements that went out to you on this meeting. Let me dispose of them before you break for the watershed.

1. What should be the relationship between the agency and the ad department of the client?

Well, which client and what agency?

If the agency executes only one play well—the end run —the answer is: guarded.

If the ad manager is one of that dying breed, the guy who pretends he is doing the agency's job, thinking his management will reward him for not getting from his agency what they are paying for, then my advice to the agency is don't wait until third down. Pass as soon as you get the ball.

But the real answer is, of course, that the relationship that succeeds best is the one where the ad manager is administrator, coordinator and approver, and the agency is originator and executor.

160

2. Should the agency have contact with the client sales and executive management?

Of course. How *much,* depends upon the management. How much can they afford? How much can they contribute?

Of course . . . unless . . .

Unless the agency isn't on the same wave length as the management, and then you have a problem that isn't going to be solved for either the agency or the client by keeping people in separate pens.

3. Is it realistic to accept the agency as a full partner and to provide the agency with confidential information knowing that some day the agency may be working for a competitor?

I don't know. You have to know the people we're talking about.

This is the damnedest business for gossip. The newspapers run special columns with Walter Winchell type trivia about the advertising business, but not about lawyers, doctors, insurance men, bankers and the like all of whom get and lose business and people and the like. Somehow I think it would be hard for the Gallagher letter to survive in the chemical industry, or machine tool industry. So maybe as a class we shouldn't be trusted.

But I don't really think that. Without notes, I could for 15 minutes straight name advertising agency people, advertising managers and media people I trust implicitly. I think we do have a problem to build into all advertising people a greater respect for the confidential than many of them have, but the pros in our business are beyond suspicion.

I guess, if you've got an agency you can't trust with confidential information you ought to be glad if they wind up with a competitor. Thereby you gain a unique competitive advantage—that of encouraging the opposition to screw up by following your mistakes.

So you see, this is like most other speeches—cheer, cheer for old Notre Dame, and take off your hat when you pass Whistler's mother.

But that's the way it is. If the right client and the right agency and the right medium get together, a hell of an exciting thing takes place and nobody ever remembers who suggested what first, and nobody worries about who is agent of whom since everybody is working for everyone else to some extent and everybody is certainly working for the advertiser, and nobody worries much about the method of compensation, only if it is too much or too little, and if it is you don't have convulsions, you have a conference.

As I said, I was asked to tell you about our gripes about client practices, publication practices and profit problems.

We have no client gripes in general and if we did it could only be because we were mad-at-the-world types. When we have a client gripe, it is with a client first person singular, and we either do something about it or we don't, depending upon the importance of it, the duration of it, and I would freely admit, depending upon our courage.

When we get mad at a publication or one of their reps, which happens, it is usually not generic and we deal with the people involved. I used to make speeches before media groups telling them what was wrong with them, but I cut that out years ago. It never did *us* any good and the people we were mad at never came to the meetings.

As to profit, this is a terrible problem, just as in your company. But it isn't up to McGraw-Hill or Clark Equipment or somebody to solve our profit problem and I totally reject the theory that a client must "guarantee" the agency a profit. Some agencies, like some companies, are well run and will keep an orderly financial house and attack the profit problem, which is as old as the profit motive, both internally and externally in specific cases. Other agencies, like other companies, will squander any added income in loose living and that's the story of the human race. I just don't happen to be particularly hot for the welfare state.

As a last gasp, there is one thing I'd like to say for adver-

tising agencies. Most of them are pretty good, and they have many values, but one of them is so evident it is almost forgotten.

Agencies are full time in the advertising business, and clients are not, so there is sometimes a difference in values. To the president of a machine tool company, advertising is only one function. To an agency man, advertising is the end product. This difference in values can be a source of agency-client misunderstanding, or it can be, as it is in an increasing number of cases, the cornerstone of a powerful partnership.

HOW TO GET THE MOST OUT OF YOUR "AD AGENCY"

Let's face the facts. Many companies simply do not get full value from their advertising agencies. All too often there's a cold war between the agency people and the client people.

It's high time, in many cases, that all pretenses were dropped—that agency and client got together to do a basic job of selling more of the client's products.

This calls for clearing up communications, sharpening up semantics, strengthening liaison, improving understanding. Most of all, it demands an enlightened attitude toward the agency and the work it does.

The client that gets full value from his agency buys not subservience but strength. No prospective client has ever asked us, "Will you do exactly as we say?" Rather, they want an assurance of experience, imagination, interest, maturity, judgment, dedication.

This is what the client buys; this is what the agency, if it is to have a successful relationship, must deliver.

163

The client pays the bill and puts its name on the promotion the public sees. The ultimate responsibility is with the advertiser. It can hire and fire agencies at will. It can accept or reject or modify proposed plans. It can exercise these functions skillfully or arbitrarily, wisely or wastefully, with understanding—or it can be completely capricious.

It is usually said that, properly, the agency's first responsibility is to its client. This is one of the reasons often given by the commission-system skeptics that the current method of payment of agencies is wrong. It is my firm belief that the way the agency is paid has nothing to do with the discharge of its responsibilities to the client—because its paramount responsibility is to itself.

The agency that serves its clients best is the one with the principles and courage to be sure that the promotion it prepares and places is honest, in good taste, representative of its best abilities, and is the kind of advertising it would run if it were held fully liable for the success or failure of the plan.

To shift responsibility to the client—to say "we had to do it this way because the client insisted on it"—is a one-way ticket to trouble.

Client-agency relationships come in all sizes, shapes and temperatures. They always start out with considerable confidence on both sides that a fine thing has happened to both companies. A deplorable number of these marriages are in trouble even before the honeymoon is over. Why?

Well, first of all there is a small but identifiable group of advertisers who are divorce-prone.

And there is a small but noisy number of agencies who are turnover-prone.

No speech or article is going to change them much. If corporations were people, they would be found in and out of the Park Avenue psychiatrists' offices. Being unsure of themselves, unable to solve their own problems first, they live in the constant hope of a new wonder drug of marketing. Statistically a minority, their comings and goings in the advertising columns unfortunately make instability somehow seem acceptable in the advertising business. In this group,

unfortunately, are a fair number of incurables, and equally unfortunately, there are no laws through which they can be effectively confined.

Then there are the client-agency breakups that are inevitable—competitive conflicts, agencies and advertisers whose operations have changed, mergers, deaths—all the normal workings of business. Nothing to do about them.

But it is the last group—the unhappy split of solid advertiser and competent agency—that deserves careful attention.

This piece is supposed to suggest to the client what he can do to be sure he gets his money's worth out of the agency of his choice. Before we go on to that, I should say that after nearly 25 years divided almost equally between being a client and an agent, I am convinced that more than half the job of building a sound relationship rests with the agency and that in more than half the cases of failure the fault started with the agency. How the agency can prevent disintegration is, however, another subject.

Seldom does trouble erupt all at once over some big, sweeping disagreement over a major policy. Nine out of ten times, if you dig out the uncomfortable facts, the blowup comes when a whole pile of petty little irritations are ignited by just one more inflammatory incident.

Also, there is one more condition that is almost a constant in these affairs. Both the marriage and the divorce are between the top executives of the two companies but the bickering is among the other members of the families. And this leads to the first two recommendations to clients who would like to build stable, rewarding relationships with their agencies:

1. *Maintain Top-Level Liaison Between the Two Companies at All Times*

The president, and always the top marketing executive of the client, should insist on knowing and seeing the principal executives of the agency, including his account supervisor, at regular intervals.

Why don't they? Only two reasons: (a) they're too busy,

on either side; or (b) insecure advertising managers or account executives try to prevent it.

Proper planning and acceptance of responsibility will cure the first. The second is trickier.

There are plenty of account executives who dislike contact by their own management, based on the false feeling that it undermines their status or exposes their mistakes.

And there are at least as many status-seeking advertising managers who stand between their agency and their marketing and management heads. Human nature being what it is, the advertising manager who isn't given status by his management will try to create it for himself, sometimes at the company's expense in terms of damming up the flow of corporate philosophy and sales realities that are the basis of every sustained good advertising program ever written.

2. *Give Your Advertising Manager Status and Authority*

If you can't, you need a new advertising manager. Unless you have an advertising manager with the ability and judgment to be a part of "management," you're wasting advertising dollars.

And if the advertising manager does have status and authority and he's still afraid to expose his advertising agency to the rest of management, you need a new agency.

The advertising manager who is insecure competes with his agency, and in any competition there is a certain amount of friction.

The advertising manager who *is* a manager leads his agency, stimulates it, encourages it and judges it.

The advertising manager who is only a corporate function stymies his agency, frustrates it, discourages it, loses its respect and is judged by it.

Read enough advertising and you can see the product of this kind of a situation. The ads are tired and trite. They seem to be written to a formula to meet a deadline.

Strong advertising managers and strong agencies fertilize and strengthen each other. If either is weak, as in Mendel's law, dwarfed issue results.

166

3. *Give Your Agency Enough Time to Work*

Once in a while an invention is born in a flash of inspiration. Usually, however, it's preceded by long patience, large dollars, and a great deal of work—often painstaking and monotonous.

The flash of great creativity comes just as seldom in advertising. Of the two dozen campaigns we are most proud of, not a one came into being full-blown. They were evolutionary. They were improvements on improvements. They were researched. They were nurtured. And all this takes time and money.

Don't be afraid to try something new. Expect your agency to keep innovating. Don't feel obligated to continue a campaign which doesn't live up to hopes. Don't expect your agency to be right every time, but be sure that the chances for success are good always. Don't give up something which is good too soon. Don't ask for great ads; insist instead on great campaigns. Don't make your agency a fire station, playing cards until the alarm rings, then improvising frantically. Keep it busy every day, working always for good promotion today, better promotion tomorrow.

4. *Hold Your Agency Responsible Only for That Which It Controls*

The greatest advertising agency in the world cannot, through the most brilliant advertising, overcome the handicaps of sales or product weaknesses.

Between sales objectives and advertising objectives there is often a great gap. If you set up, jointly, measurable advertising objectives, you will have a fair and sound basis of evaluation. Fly-by-night client-agency relationships are often the outgrowth of fly-by-night objectives.

5. *Be Realistic about Agency Production Costs*

Even sophisticated and otherwise understanding clients sometimes misunderstand agency production charges.

There seems to be a widely held belief that agencies live

167

loosely when it comes to either print or radio-TV production. The facts, I am certain, are almost always quite the opposite.

After talking with hundreds of printers, engravers, art studios, package producers and others, I am firmly convinced that, on the whole, agencies are much tighter buyers than advertisers themselves. So how come the problem?

First, agencies must buy the best. They cannot safely gamble with quality. Their reputation, not the printer's or the engraver's, is on the line. So the client who gives some of his business to the printer down the street sees prices that are not really for comparable work. You can overgeneralize on this point, but there is much substance in fact.

Second, and far more important, the agency's price includes the cost of overhead for interviewing suppliers, getting quotations, issuing purchase orders, supervising the job, billing, etc. Our production people are out part of every week working with suppliers while client's jobs are running, watching quality.

The advertiser can do this himself, and if he handles production on his own, he usually does. If he has equally competent people doing the job, he pays the same basic salaries. But he seldom adds on the overhead when he compares prices.

Agency overhead ranges from around 125% to 185%, depending mostly upon location. This covers the familiar rent, light, heat, social security, insurance—all the normal fixed-expense items. The advertiser has his overhead rate, too. From a dozen studies I've examined, it appears to be somewhat higher, actually, than that of the typical agency. We have many clients with overhead rates of 200% to 300%.

Few advertisers remember to add overhead to the costs of handling the production they do themselves. But it is inevitably there. Put it on your own costs, and now make the comparison. Those advertisers who have done so have had an eye-opening experience.

The typical agency buys more printing, more engraving,

more art, more talent than any of its clients (again, with some few exceptions). If it buys stupidly, it is a stupid agency.

6. *Expect Your Agency to Make a Profit on Your Account*

If you want your agency to give its ungrudging best, be sure it is making money. We work in a competitive economy; good agencies make good profits and want to make better ones.

Cost-plus agency service bothers me. The more service, the more profits. Is this good? Would you be happy rewarding inefficiency? Do you want to pay more for fumbling than for incisive action?

Hourly based fees, at least as an exclusive compensation, bother me. They are subject to the same abuses as cost-plus. The incentive for greater profit is a powerful client lever for better agency performance. The client that doesn't use it misses a real bet in getting more for his advertising dollars.

Want to shake up your agency? Ask it this:

"How can you double your profit on our account without increasing our costs, while at the same time increasing the effectiveness of our advertising?"

That's a business-like challenge. A good agency will take it seriously. It's a serious, confidence-building question.

7. *Treat Your Agency Like a Business Partner*

This is the point on which all other papers on this subject, whether by client or agency, seem to start. This is where we quit.

Actually, it's a summary. It's a generalization, completely correct, but it needs to be implemented to be meaningful. Do the other six things, and your agency won't have to ask to be a partner. It will be one—in sales meetings, in budget presentations, in field calls—in all the other things that make it automatically say "we" instead of "you."

Assuming, of course, that having been given this opportunity, your agency earns the right to keep it.

MUST THE CALENDAR RULE ADVERTISING?

I wish there were some way to outlaw January 1 in the advertising business. The cycle of the calendar does more damage to good sales and advertising plans than any other single factor.

Because every year that magic date January 1, comes along sales plans are scrapped, budgets are rewritten, advertising campaigns are changed or stopped short, and there is a frantic flight into creative outer space to "come up with something different."

But not always something better.

Companies have to file an annual tax return, and therefore make annual forecasts, annual summaries, annual reports to stockholders, and so on. But sales and advertising cycles are seldom exactly 12 months.

We handle a good many agricultural accounts. Sales patterns tend to be seasonal, not annual. On the other hand, clients who manufacture capital goods may have a more nearly annual selling pattern because purchases may be influenced by depreciation or tax considerations; but even then, big capital purchases (power-plant equipment, pipelines, process plants, for instance) are several years in the making.

The trouble with the calendar is that it doesn't take the real sales considerations into effect. Some companies ought to make five-month budgets or nine-month budgets. Others really ought to make two-year budgets or 37-month budgets, or whatever is best for them.

At least the sales plans ought to be built that way, and therefore advertising plans ought to be built that way.

The worst waste in advertising is dropping a successful campaign just when it is beginning to build an audience or increase inquiries or influence direct sales.

Stopping advertising campaigns yearly and starting over is like reading half of a mystery story and then starting a

new one—you never know for sure how it will come out. The purpose is never quite fulfilled.

We know all these things so well. We've seen case after case, haven't we, where the sales message is beginning to be played back just as the manufacturer abandons it?

Really good sales ideas, for any company or any product, are scarce. Once identified, they need long exposure. A new idea may easily be a weaker idea. The best salesmen may modify and adapt but they don't desert a successful sales proposition.

What can we do about it?

About the annual *budget,* perhaps we can't do much— the odds are with the public accountants and the Internal Revenue Service.

About the annual *plans,* we can do a good deal if it means enough to make the effort. We can present sales and advertising programs that are cycled to the market, not to the calendar. If they must then be broken into shorter segments, or expanded to longer-range financial plans, that can be done, as long as the *total plan* is the basic recommendation.

Here and there, the most sophisticated marketers are beginning to realize the profit potential in sales cycles instead of time cycles.

If January 1 has to be a time for good resolutions, I'd suggest that the number-one resolution be to build *selling* programs that fit the realities of *selling,* and then and only then break the dollar programs into the realities of the inevitable audit and tax programs.

Creativity

Of all the functions of advertising, the one that has interested Bill Marsteller the most and on which he has spent most of his time by far is creativity. During the early days of his agency, he was a prolific writer of advertising. His experiences in those days with the agency was the basis for a speech on "How to Develop Creativity in a Smaller Agency," which was made before advertising industry meetings in the Southwest and on the West Coast, where agencies tend to be small.

His early days as an advertising writer were predominantly in the industrial field, and in the second speech, reprinted here, on "Creative Trends in Industrial Advertising," he looks back on the changes that have taken place in this broad area of advertising activity.

HOW TO DEVELOP CREATIVITY
IN THE SMALLER AGENCY

One of the occasional interests of the advertising trade press is the future of the small agency.

It is sort of a foolish and repetitive finger exercise in an unchanging key, but, as you know, there's a period between year-end round-ups and the smelt run of spring conventions when everybody is busy getting out the year's ads and no one says anything controversial.

An easily prepared filling to go around the media ads in the advertising press is a re-examination of the plight of the small agency.

This generally colorless and odorless story points out that the small agency has a hard lot competing with the big boys on even grounds in research, media buying clout, computerized market-matching, recruiting, training, merchandising, overseas offices, test kitchens, captive consumer panels, and corporate aircraft.

Then it points out that it costs relatively little to start a new advertising agency, therefore many people try it, and that the incidence of failure is very high, but a handful make it, and this is very good because how could we have big agencies if we didn't have small ones first, and this is very American, or, at least, very Texan.

Then, asks the story of itself, what characterizes this

tiny group of tiny agencies that makes it through puberty? CREATIVITY!

That has to be it, for a great mind is a great thing and very personal, and, as Edison proved, you can invent for yourself better than for the System, and only a spoilsport would even remember that Steinmetz invented for General Electric and Kettering for General Motors.

Anyway, so the story goes, Little David was small but oh my, he slew Big Goliath, who lay down and dieth, buried under his research reports and profit statements from branch offices, while David triumphantly waves aloft a two-word headline and a new type face.

The theory goes that while the little agency may be enormously handicapped by the shorts in eleven out of twelve departments, since creativity is the name of the game, and since patents are issued to individuals, the little agency with one or two truly inventive people can compete on even grounds with J. Walter Erickson. Maybe even more so, since it doesn't have all these forms to fill out, and all these meetings to go to, and all these committees to stamp out verbal and visual Spam.

Well, my friends, it just isn't so, in my opinion. I think it is twice as hard for a little agency to be creative as a big one. The only reason a lot of small agencies *are* as creative as big ones is because there isn't any alternative.

But it isn't easy. It's hard; damned hard.

I know. We will have been in business short of two decades, and we have been a small agency most of that time. I grant you that these things are comparative, and some of you may think of us as a big agency, but I find that very funny. Big is what clients are, not agencies. And even among agencies, there are some with more people in one department than we have in a whole office.

So what I'm trying to say is that we are as familiar as you with the problems of running a small agency.

Creativity is one of them.

It doesn't even come first with the typical small agency. Too bad, but true.

176

Check me if this isn't so: with only one or two principals certain other things have a time priority—finance and accounting, hiring and firing, client contact. There's no personnel department, no controller's division, no management service representatives to turn things over to. The fire department is all volunteer and has no special uniform.

These are not the ingredients of a creative climate.

Leo Burnett can turn over management matters to some others, if he chooses, and block out the time to create. So can Bill Bernbach, Fax Cone, and George Gribben, as indeed they all have. Not so the head of a five-man shop in Denver, let us say. His first problem is to stay in business and I tell you with the chill of the event still in my bones that the worry, the fatigue, the involvement of simply keeping the business moving ahead is not the classic climate of invention.

The big agency, it seems to me, has so many advantages that I wonder that you and I have been able to do so well, relatively, in competing with them on the creative front. They can, if they choose, departmentalize, delegate, set up creative task forces, move their bright people around to lead and teach. We, alas, often have to be generalists.

Alas?

The truth, I think, is that the strength of the small agency is in its very character as a marketing or communications generalist. I think that the small agency can build an over-all client empathy and intimacy, an over-all usefulness to the client, that the large agency with its specialists and division of labor is hard-put to achieve, especially if the client is also fairly small.

The little agency has a focal point, and that's a big, big advantage.

The principal of the small agency is often a total businessman. Being an entrepreneur as well as a craftsman, he can identify with the entrepreneur.

I believe that at the core of the success of the small agencies that have grown rapidly you will usually find a man, or a couple of men, with an instinctive sense for run-

177

ning a business. I have no special insight into what made Doyle Dane Bernbach a great success, but based on interviews with several of their people I have been unable to hire, I would bet that Mr. Dane, who is not reputed to be a creative man, had at least as much to do with the development of that fine company as did Mr. Bernbach, who is obviously an enormously talented creator.

Yet finally, as Mr. Burnett has often observed, someone has to get out the ads. And finally, no matter how well run, your agency and ours will be judged on the excellence of the product, seen and heard.

And here's the rub. It takes extraordinary effort and self-discipline for the small, modestly financed agency to be bright and fresh and imaginative while at the same time staying fiscally seaworthy. The fat float easily, but the thin have to kick a little.

We know the problem. We have lived with it for 15 years. The rest of this talk will list what has come out of our fumbling, sometimes failing, efforts to nurture and polish and elevate our creativity. So let us now together rediscover the wheel.

First, let me give you five suggestions that aren't directly concerned with creativity at all. They are designed merely to tidy up the joint so that creativity can breathe.

Number one, make your open door policy figurative not literal until you get big enough to afford someone who can sit around with his door open and his couch dusted, inviting interruptions. Doors, we tell our people, were made to be closed, so that people can be alone, doing things that people do best alone, like thinking, writing, or drawing. There is this crazy idea abroad in business today that you only shut the door when you are firing someone or playing jiggery-pokey with the books. Anybody who has invention as a part of his job description is entitled to periods of rigid non-interruption and isolation.

The second step toward creativity, we think, is clear, defoliated job descriptions. Too many people in this business are creating who shouldn't be creating, especially in

178

small agencies. Creating should be left to people who have creating clearly included in their job descriptions.

Third, we would suggest that you run a couple of training meetings a year, every year, on the use of time. There are books and articles on this subject, and some are better than others, but no matter; any of them are good enough to serve as texts for a couple of one-hour meetings a year. You will want to remind your people (and yourself) of the ways to reduce dictating time, how to build work agendas, what to throw away unread, how to write conference reports, how to get the most out of your secretary—always a popular discussion—and how to hold friendly, relaxed interviews within a tight time schedule.

Fourth, we find it useful to review all routine procedures once a year and see how many we can simplify or eliminate. For instance, for years we avoided a traffic department and the work a normal traffic department does was divided between the account man's secretary and the media department, eliminating one level of communication and responsibility, and about three tons of reports to be written, read, corrected, fouled-up, and marked for filing.

Fifth, we've had good experience by using consultants for many of the noncreative management and administrative jobs. Our basic budget system was set up by a professor of business administration, and he continues his quarterly review of our performance. We've used all kinds of consultants for all kinds of research. This has held down fixed costs, given us merchandisable names, and greatly reduced the time the principals have spent on methodology and research procurement. When we've expanded or rented new offices we've usually used consultants to minimize executive involvement. When we have needed a head candler or a fashion expert we have rented them, until we were big enough to own our own.

The only things we don't use consultants for much is hiring people and for doing the creative job.

People, because that's our business, and we want in-house control of it. Totally. But that's another speech.

Creative, because that's our product, but it won't be ours if we job much of it out to free-lancers and contract thinkers.

Now let me suggest six things a little more directly concerned with creativity we have found helpful in improving our creative product.

First, use art directors to their creative capacity. Just as an experienced copy man thinks visually as well as verbally, a good art director thinks in ideas which match words with pictures or sound. Long ago we concluded it was false economy to hire art directors at low cost. Good art directors are not content merely to be renderers, and if you structure your art department that way we believe you are wasting a great potential resource. Art directors often become excellent headline writers, we find. Art directors think in campaign concepts. Art directors have creative thinking time while they are at the drawing board and the trick is to get them to use that time thinking about fresh advertising ideas instead of a fresh approach to your secretary. So we say to art directors, in effect, "Try harder. Go beyond pictures. Create advertising, not layouts."

Second, habitualize the time for creation.

Let me explain. Like most little agencies we started without a copy department. The contact man wrote his own copy, or perhaps more accurately in our case, the copy man was responsible for contact. Most agencies, as they grow, abandon this system. We never have, although we now have creative directors and handle many accounts with a division of copy and contact. But many of our people still have the problem of shifting back and forth between doing and dreaming. It is a very demanding way of life.

Our best people have learned to habitualize the creative period. How they do it varies, but let me give you a couple of examples. One man writes every Tuesday, eight in the morning until five at night, come Hell or high water, and no one goes near him. On Monday evening his office is made ready like a bridal chamber. Everything he is going to need is at hand—every bit of reference material, all product

180

data, paper, pencils, fresh typewriter ribbon, and so on. His lunch on Tuesday never changes and is automatically delivered at noon. He is among our most engaging people, but on Tuesday evening he is a bastard.

Another man, who once a month turns out a very well-done house organ, does it in one sitting, every fourth Sunday morning, at home. Another man likes to get three or four people together and talk the problem to death. Then he writes a half-dozen or more headlines on separate sheets and carries them around with him. For a couple of weeks he writes unrelated sentences, words, ideas on each, as the trial headlines may suggest. Finally, he locks himself up and writes, in one sitting, three, four or five ads. The result is good.

The point is, of course, to get into the habit of creating in a certain way, without interference, within an established environment that leaves little excuse for doing anything other than creating.

Third, we believe the smaller agency must be especially certain to establish creative review procedures. When manpower is limited there is a great temptation to go from rough copy and layout direct to client approval without built-in checks to be sure that the work is up to the agency's standards.

Beyond this, we do several things in the way of after-the-fact critical review. We have an internal critique, called "Sticks & Stones," loosely modeled after the New York Times' "Winners and Sinners," in which we praise good work and gently reprove the less good. Outstanding work is publicly applauded, naming names.

Fourth, we have continual training in creativity. Externally we send people to the several commercial creative seminar-type meetings, some of which are good and some not, but they do give us another way to show that we are serious about trying to upgrade creativity. Internally, we have finally developed some techniques of training that seem to work. They involve the creative attack on a hypothetical advertising situation. Often we use a new business

opportunity as the vehicle for creative training. Beyond this, the training program takes two or more groups of two to four people each, and gives them the same problem to develop into a finished advertising campaign. Then each group presents its program to the agency management and to each other, after which there is analytical discussion. We have often brought in outsiders with appropriate qualifications to sit in on the discussions. We do these exercises after hours, or in the summer months when the space salesmen are touring Europe.

Another part of our creative training plan is the exposure of our people to mind-stretching thought leaders. We bring them in to talk on a variety of nonadvertising subjects. We care less about their subject matter than that they are stimulating and willing to engage in a no-holds-barred discussion. As examples, since the first of the year we have had Dr. Donald Taylor of Yale and Dr. Milton Rokeach of Michigan State who are doing research into creativity; Dr. John Kouwenhoven, an author and English professor at Barnard; a senior editor of TIME; the chairman of the board of one of our larger clients; Dean James Hayes of Duquesne, an expert on self-development; and an officer of the Federal Reserve System.

The fifth of these last points is that in a small agency, even more than in a big one, you need to reward creativity. In a big, departmentalized agency a creative man can progress through several levels and, still in the creative department there are promotions to challenge him. Further, he can find personal fulfillment in the praise of the other creative people around him, and I think you will agree that this matter of recognition is very important to most creative people.

By contrast, in the small agency the creative man frequently can only be promoted to general management, and he may not have that kind of talent. There is no auditorium full of other artists or copywriters to applaud him; his recognition must come from you and from me, and we mustn't forget to give it.

Obviously there are titles and money at your disposal, but standing alone they are too pat an answer. We believe that the small agency has an exceptional advantage in being able to include creative people in the fundamental decisions of management. When you are small, when the key people can have lunch at one table, it is easier to instill togetherness; when you get bigger, participation has to be programmed.

On working quarters. We don't believe in copywriter cubbyholes or art bull pens. We believe that creativity is individual and creative people should be treated as individuals.

On money, I think it is very hard to pirate a happy creative man with mere money. Two New York agencies with fine creative credits are not paying the highest salaries in town. But their people are loath to leave a climate that honors and cherishes them.

And this, then, brings us to the last point.

In the small agency or the large one, we believe you have to upgrade creativity by pulling it up from the top, not pushing it up from the bottom.

A creative climate, we believe, is established by the agency heads. We think management has to want great advertising fully as much as it wants great profits if ultimately it is to have either. Creative plans boards and creative review procedures will be only as important as management makes them.

No agency is so small that in one way or another it is impossible to delegate some of the other problems at least enough so that the creative function gets some visible attention every day.

It's hard to keep the creative people juiced up every day in a small agency. Consider just the little fact of proximity: if Marion Harper came in bilious and bleary in the morning, who knew it? If the small agency head comes in bitchy, by 9:30 the word is out that it's a bad day at Black Rock. The account types have a choice: they can go to a client, hoping that he wasn't out with the boss last night. But the creative

183

people are stuck in the office, nervous and tense, and useful invention is shot for the day.

Really, when you come down to it, running a small agency is an intensely personal thing. The kind of agency you or I will have will probably be a pretty fair replica of the kind of people we are, and what we want most, and like best and stand for.

There are a lot of good, fine things to stand for, but if you want to have a creative agency, probably you'd better stand for creativity way up top. Not just in the preamble to the new business pitch, not just in a corporate emblem designed to suggest infinity, not just by putting it first in the policy manual, but by living that way. As Mr. Coué said, every day, in every way, getting better and better.

And there's one nice thing about living this way—about putting the development of creative excellence above all else:

It's the most fun.

CREATIVE TRENDS IN INDUSTRIAL
ADVERTISING

The trouble with spending most of your life in one industry is that by the time you have finally figured out what it is all about, it's all changed.

This sure isn't the same business I got into 25 years ago.

I look back and see no good old days. As recently as 25 years ago industrial advertising was the ghetto of management; the lower east side of the communications business.

Industrial advertising was not integrated into the total advertising community. True, there was tokenism: The Association of National Advertisers usually handed out one directorship to the industrials, so that for their taxes the peasants would have the illusion of representation. The American Association of Advertising Agencies maintained

a carefully subjugated committee on Business Papers, but the majority of its membership was drawn from among the faceless young trainees in the media departments of the big consumer houses.

The business paper publishers, when you think back, were pretty arrogant. With pious puritanism they told us to read their trade papers because it was good for us. They had a mission, they said, to serve their industries and we had an obligation to support them.

They ground out spineless, odorless, colorless issue after issue, and when anyone suggested that maybe people weren't reading their unkempt meanderings, he was told he didn't understand the special disciplines of editing to technical audiences.

They issued such circulation statements as pleased them, and when we suggested that we would like audits, and audits that were independent, comparable, and covered both paid and free, we were treated as treacherous antagonists, rather than valued customers.

It all seems so strange today when even the newest business school graduate understands that the success of a venture is in the hands of the buyer, but that failure is in the hands of the seller.

What was even worse was the advertising.

I have recently gone back over some of the first campaigns I did. I am astonished that I could have ever been so naïve, so willing to follow the bad advice we were being given, so unable to adapt the writing, psychology, and art courses I had had in school, so quick with a cliché when an idea came slowly, so utterly, utterly, utterly dull.

We were conditioned to that kind of advertising. The big gimmick in industrial advertising was "Tell All." ABP, perhaps to draw attention away from the problem it was having maintaining its postage subsidy, put a lot of promotion dollars behind this proposition which in short held that you did not sell your machine tool until you had explained exactly how you manufactured each part that went into it.

185

With great pride.

In small type.

This was followed by a big campaign that told all of us who were writing industrial advertising that we should "Follow the Editors."

The weakness in this advice is apparent in rereading some of the bibles of the industry of those days. Mostly, the editors had no idea where they were going.

Yet in the last ten years we've come so far. The best trade papers are now very good indeed, and getting better. As they do, time is running out for the parasitic publisher who has quietly sucked away promotion dollars to no end but his own.

What is best of all is the enormous improvement in creativity in industrial advertising. Today, the best trade paper advertising has reached parity with excellent consumer advertising.

It is this development—the growing trend toward creativity in industrial advertising—that I want you to consider with me for the rest of this talk.

There are two groups of influences, I think, that have pulled creativity up so far so fast. The first group comes from what is happening in the marketplace and from the growing literature on the art of marketing. The second group comes out of the practice of advertising itself. First, let's look at the marketing influences.

1. *Systems Selling*

Industrial marketing today is much more complex, made so by complex technologies and by complicated ways of looking at problems. The man who once said, "I need a ¾ in. bolt," now says, "I need a way of fastening these parts." Warner Swasey used to sell turret lathes: today it sells a system of machining. Professor Theodore Levitt of Harvard, who needs to be read over and over if we are to understand some of the things that are going on in marketing, says that today it is often not the product we are selling but the proposition.

186

This whole concept has freed the creator of industrial advertising. He has escaped from the moldy straitjacket of "tell-all" advertising. He is encouraged to invent. He is able to write to the buyer instead of the seller.

2. *Turnkey Selling*

Once, if you built a power plant, you or your engineering firm assembled all the materials and parts. Now, if you'll let them, several companies will contract to do the whole thing and turn over to you the key to a going operation. In less extreme and increasingly common circumstances, a machine tool manufacturer will give you a whole assembly line, or a regulator builder a whole control system.

This has done something to advertising, too. The same people aren't interested in the same things. The ultimate user is less interested in the details of the subsuppliers' products; he still, however, has to have respect for the sub-supplier company.

More and more industrial advertising, even for quite small companies, is image-building or institutional rather than product sell.

3. *Automated Purchasing*

This is a development that is scaring some marketers so badly they are starting to go back to church again. It takes many forms, but in essence it assumes that once I get on your approved list, my orders come automatically from your computer as it discovers that your inventory is low. In the ultimate, your computer and my computer handle all this untouched by human hands and uncorrupted by human emotions. Or human corruption. This clarifies the purchasing function as what it really always has been—a risk reduction process.

Therefore, buying becomes a series of big human decisions, followed by thousands of small machine decisions. The big decisions will be made by big men, high placed, in committees, difficult to see.

Could it be that big men read big ads? Some of our smartest creators seem to think so.

4. *Product Life Cycle*

So much has been written about this and it all sums up in one word. Shorter.

Technology and modern communications combine to get products accepted more quickly, copied more quickly and replaced more quickly.

So the creative advertising man doesn't have time for love play. Today is the day. The time is now.

5. *Selective Selling*

We know much more about the companies and the men in them who make up our market today. Mostly again, thank the computer, but also the imaginative men in publishers, agencies and advertisers who are recognizing the possibilities of selective selling. There are new media breakdowns to identify selected, prevalued audiences. Watered direct mail lists are getting dried out. Promotion can now be written to the individual, instead of to the average.

6. *Allocation of Resources*

We have always had the choice, given a budget of X amount, of spending it on trade papers, consumer publications, trade shows, catalogs, publicity, radio, and so on, in any combination of any amounts. Our decisions were compounded of the past, prejudice, pressure, and politics.

For most of us this is still true, but not for long. Lots of quiet experimentation is going on in marketing simulation and the development of marketing matrices to test out various combinations, and it may turn out after all these years that another page of space *is* better than another case of whiskey for the Kansas City salesman. Of course it may not, too.

But the upshot will be that the ultimate allocation of resources will have all communications working together,

not conceived and executed by separate people for separate objectives, sometimes jealously defended against reason.

The Marketing Concept

Finally, over all, and above all else, we are influenced by the age of the Marketing Concept.

The motto is now, "Let the Seller Beware!"

The great successes of today are not alone technological. They occur when a company combines technological excellence with marketing excellence. When a company quits thinking, as Ted Levitt urges, about being in the railroad business and instead says it is in transportation. Or when a company quits thinking of itself as a manufacturer and instead as a problem-solver. Like IBM.

The marketing concept has done great things for advertising creativity, consumer and industrial. It has given advertising new meaning, new purpose, new direction. It has made stuffy, self-serving advertising seem outdated and petty and ridiculous. It has caused young men to write better and think more clearly, and old men to retire early.

At the same time that these marketing influences have been at work reshaping the thinking of the creative man, there have been at least three major advertising influences affecting his style.

1. *New Graphic Processes*

At long last, trade papers are beginning to awaken to the possibilities of new graphic processes. It should have happened ten years ago, but too many trade paper publishers, accustomed to looking backward and protecting the old way of life, missed the opportunity. The few who looked ahead did grave damage to their competition and now, with more open-minded men heading some of the big trade paper houses, the stampede to offset printing and cheap color is likely to simply run over any holdouts.

New typesetting methods, new photographic processes and new printing procedures are available to let the creative man use nearly any communications technique he chooses.

If the Stone Age union heads in the graphic arts fields will let us, we will revolutionize printed communications in our lifetime.

2. *Consumer Advertising*

At all points in the history of industrial advertising concurrent consumer advertising has been brighter, warmer and more successful. At all times the industrial ad man was exposed to it, just as he is today, and presumably he could learn. But the cartel told us to look the other way—that the purchasing agent was a cold, calculating, sober, sexless logician when he read his business paper.

Of course, it was a little hard to explain away the goings-on at the annual convention of the National Association of Purchasing Agents, not to mention the annual stag of the local chapters, but that was the party line.

Now we have more research to guide us, and more different kinds, and what do you know, purchasing agents and chief engineers and accountants are human and are reached and moved and stimulated the same way as normal people.

So we get no black marks any more for imitating consumer advertising.

3. *Media Flexibility*

Not only has the computer made it easier for us to identify our true prospects, but the best of our media are making it possible for us to promote to them through partial buys and special editions determined by geographic occupation or even plant or income size.

Now, in the remaining minutes, let's take all these influences, mix them together, and see what kind of creative trends they are generating.

If you read your trade books carefully, you must be aware of the snowballing use of full color.

Once over half of the magazines were in two colors. Research began to make us aware that a second color often produced fewer readers than black and white. Now we are really moving, really reaching out, with live, dramatic, beautifully printed color.

We've learned to hit hard, too. With short product life, with corporate-wide selling, with a new appreciation that marketing is a language of verbs, present tense and promise, we've learned the power of impact.

There are many ways to get impact, of course. The most common one is to buy a lot of space, but a lot of space, big words, tightly-cropped pictures aren't the only way. Art can do it for you, too. And really good photography.

As you study the leading business papers of today, you begin to realize that the art director is much more involved in the creative process than he used to be. The day when the copywriter, account man or client handed a renderer a pencil layout to clean up is pretty well over. Pictures are at least as important as words today. In fact, this is the day of the big picture.

For years, we have been taught that we should think in campaigns, that ads must have a rigid family appearance, and that you should aim at a "feel" so that even if the audience doesn't read the ad, it knows who the company is that bought the space.

Some very bright people are beginning to say that this is fine reasoning and very sound for big companies and big budgets, but that for little companies and little budgets the ultimate cost of getting your communications objectives out of a total campaign is too great, and that each ad has to stand on its own feet, making its own points individually. This theory assumes that the Polaski Ball Bearing Company, annual sales $1,500,000, all stock owned by Charlie Polaski, is not going to be able to spend enough money or have enough time to really register a Polaski family façade on the not-breathlessly-waiting audience of *Machine Design*.

This is the thinking of heretics, but research scores show that if the few ads are good they do much better than the many that aren't. Of course.

If you look back a few years into trade paper advertising you will be struck by the complexity and confusion in their construction. Today, there is an undeniable trend toward simplicity.

191

Now the attempt is to cut away extraneous elements. Simplify the signature. Peel off the gingerbread. Fire the paper hanger. Get down to the real wood. Just say what you have to say. Even couponed ads are getting defoliated.

Selective selling, as we have said, is coming in the demographic, geographical and other kinds of magazine split runs. It is also putting more imagination and a third dimension into direct mail. It is made-to-measure promotion.

When you know just who you want to reach—by name; when you are after annual order commitments; when you are confronted with the problems of penetrating the highest decision-making groups, you have to be different. You can afford to spend much more on a per-person promotion, too, when the stakes are big.

If you watch the winners of the DMAA awards you note a changing pattern. They are less likely to be brochures now, and more likely to be involved 3-D mailings, in series, with a direct relationship to the sales proposition. They tend to be campaigns that cost $20 to $150 per name and when well done pay out with measurable profitability.

These, then, are some of the clearly defined trends in industrial advertising. Some are better classified as fads, and a fad, someone has observed, is something that goes in one era and out the other.

What's happening today that isn't so visible is the considerable experimentation that is going on in visual and spoken business communications. For instance:

Several companies have developed low-cost television cameras and video tape recorders. I have already seen them used to screen a sales proposition in the manufacturer's plant, and played the same day in the prospect's office. The possibilities are unlimited.

Information retrieval systems—computer banks, microfilm and other methods—are sure to change cataloguing and are likely to have a great impact not only on the way information is stored, but the way it is communicated in the first place.

The diversified, agglomerate company, cutting across many industries, will be increasingly tempted by mass communications—television, radio, consumer magazines, or, at the very least, business-wide or science-wide publications like *Business Week* and *Scientific American.* Already, here in Los Angeles, there is a substantial expenditure in radio by industrial companies to catch the commuting engineers and managers in their automobiles.

One place to look to see what's ahead in technical communications is the medical field. Doctors have a terrible, continuing re-education problem. The ethical drug companies and medical supply companies are using all kinds of techniques to reach them, inform them, demonstrate to them.

New communications methods will father new forms of creativity. We'll deal with *all* the senses, and the imaginative promotions of the future will be the ones that combine sight, sound, touch and smell most effectively.

The art of persuasion and the art of teaching will be more and more closely allied.

Business papers may or may not any longer be printed and mailed from a central spot. In any event, they will be more different from than they will be like today's product.

The key to the future, of course, is not to think of ourselves as in the industrial advertising business or trade paper business but in business communications. It's an obvious statement, but we are conditioned to do things as we have done them, and that will be fatal in the future.

It seems likely that the distinction between industrial and consumer advertising will dim, as many techniques become interchangeable. Pretty clearly it will be the creative man who will best adapt.

For the man who loves to innovate, the man who is not afraid to doubt the past and test the future, the man who would rather have his name on a patent than a policy, it looks like a pretty good time to be around.

Editorial Evaluation

Starting in 1955, the Marsteller agency launched a long running study of media evaluation through editorial evaluation. The purpose was to put some qualitative measures on the readership of publications to supplement the quantitative measures found in audit statements.

This was the start of a campaign to look beyond the distribution of media and into media quality.

Bill Marsteller contended that the vitality of a publication started with its editor. This, needless to say, is a very popular concept among editors and, as a consequence, he has spoken before many such groups. One typical speech before a conference of magazine editors is included here.

HOW THE ADVERTISER LOOKS AT THE EDITOR

This symposium was set up to explore how publishers, advertisers, readers and editors themselves view the editor. This seems to indicate that someone thinks the editor looks different to each of these groups.

If so, I submit to you that the whole discussion is based on a false premise.

It seems perfectly apparent to me that the editor can be viewed in only one way by anyone—as the man who determines whether or not the publication has any right to exist.

It is the editor who determines if readers, in sufficient numbers, will bother to open the magazine in the first place and then proceed through it with sufficient interest, to justify advertisers to place their messages in it.

It is the editor, therefore, who breathes life into the circulation, which without his ministering hand remains only a collection of names, like a telephone directory where there are no telephones.

I have known many editors in my day. Like advertising men, they come in all shapes and sizes and ages and some are technically competent and some are dedicated and some verge on brilliance, and some have trouble getting Band-Aids on straight after cutting themselves with their scissors, and some are distinguished largely by the caked paste they have dribbled on their neckties.

197

So generalizations about editors, like generalizations about most things, are so much verbal garbage.

I think, however, there are a few sweeping statements you can make about editors.

The first is that their publications will be about as good as they are themselves, or about as good as their publishers will let them make them.

The second is that at least a modest majority of editors think they are not appreciated.

A third is that a very great many of them are underpaid.

A fourth is that of those who are underpaid, a good many ought to be.

If this talk had a theme, I suppose it would be "Workers Arise." For you hold the destiny of your publishing houses.

It has been proven that advertising can be sold in any rag, almost literally, that anyone can put together. It may be sold on the basis of editorial puffs, or association politics, or friendship, or persistence, or reciprocity, or numbers or nearly anything else, but no publication I know has ever made very much money over a very long time without having a pretty good editorial product.

So advertising alone doesn't beget success.

I don't want to declare war on circulation managers, because God knows they feel even sorrier for themselves than editors, and they have none of the editor's warm feeling of holy semi-professionalism to fall back on, but they are not the cornerstone of successful publishing either. A wonderfully circulated but miserably edited publication goes directly to the wastebasket, adding nothing to learning or pleasure, and in fact only adding to the post office department's deficit.

But on the other hand, a brilliantly edited magazine cries out to be circulated. In the underground of World War II, dismal looking publications were smuggled from hand to hand because they contained otherwise unobtainable information, or because they set forth the mind-stretching ideas of leadership, or because they proposed a plan of action.

198

The parallel between the press of patriotism under war conditions and the press of the business world in a free economy may be a tenuous one, but the principles apply. I have known people who actually *did* walk a mile for a Camel, and I have run up a two dollar taxi bill trying to find a newsstand that hadn't sold out of the Sunday *New York Times,* and I have known men who reached first for their business paper when the mail was put on their desk, because they knew that the chances were good that the magazine would be more interesting or more informative than any of the other things in the pile.

But there are mighty few newspapers worth two dollars in taxi fare and mighty few business papers that deserve to be put on top of the pile of mail.

And it all depends on the editor.

All of this is just to build a foundation to answer the questions I'm supposed to discuss which is "How does the advertiser look at the editor?"

And you see, from what I have already said, I can't answer it. I can only ask back, "Which editor?"

Probably the reason I was asked to represent the advertiser interests on this panel is because we've been working so hard in our agency trying to build editorial evaluation into the space buying process.

This has been an eye-opening experience. Our space buyers and account executives know a great deal more about the editorial excellence or deficiencies of specific business publications than they did a few years ago because to do anything with editorial evaluation you have to open several issues of a publication and go through them rather thoroughly.

To our very great surprise, more than a few editors didn't like it. I could wade around my office up to my navel in letters from editors and publishers whose wounded cries can be summed up in the concept that only the reader can evaluate the editorial in a specialized publication, and that most certainly an advertiser can not.

This is arrant, arrogant sheep-dip. Even allowing for

the possible lower mentality of the advertiser, a fair number of them are literate, some are intellectually curious, some are quite interested in their business, many of them already are readers of specialized publications, and not a few of them have the added qualification of being writers themselves.

In fact, after four years and $50,000 worth of editorial evaluation research I get a little galled between the ears when I hear again this clap-trap that the advertiser and his agency must not presume to judge editorial quality or leadership.

It seems to me that the same reader who reads your editorial must be the man or woman who reads our advertising. At least that's what your space salesmen say. If you understand him and we don't, we must be producing a lot of wasted, unread advertising. If we don't understand him, you'd better tell us how to do so, instead of hiding your knowledge behind a patronizing dismissal of our willingness to learn.

Advertising, like editorial, is valueless unless it is read and understood.

Editing any publication is a useful and demanding business, or, if it makes you feel better, profession. It is not, however, a skill based on mystery or manual dexterity or props.

And at this point I'll digress to say that from visiting dozens of editorial offices and talking with even more editors, I've come to have a low opinion of the forced trappings of editorial direction.

For example, the schedule board. I've seen a lot of them, mostly out of date. Out-of-date schedule boards go hand-in-hand with out-of-date editors.

And the forced editorial formula. Most good cooks have read a lot of cook books, but if your wife prepares every meal with the book open on the sink beside her, you are doomed to gustatory mediocrity.

And the publisher's regular exercise in pontification on

page 3, or wherever, because the publisher always has that space.

And the special editorial treatment in depth, every June, of the growing Southeast, because every June we give depth coverage to the Southeast, there being some relationship to the fact that the sales department finds that working toward Florida once a year is best done in February and March.

I like Elmer Tangerman, because when he was a McGraw-Hill editor, without asking his publisher, he looked up one day at the schedule board, called the office boy and said, "Throw that damned thing out!"

I love the editor, who shall go nameless to protect the innocent, who threw his publisher's loving message to his industry into the wastebasket because it was mealy-mouthed and vapid, and instead filled the space with some firm recommendations for improving the relationship between that industry and a government regulatory body.

As an advertiser I suppose I ought to be glad to see this growing trend of making space salesmen into publishers. A lot of them are my friends, and pretty uniformly they are deserving, intelligent, hard working and eager. But I think that on the whole, it's a bum trend. Especially among special interest, scientific and business magazines.

When you look back over the history of publications, you will see that far the majority of the best ones came to their zenith under an editor-publisher. In recent years, there have been some significant commercial successes of publications brought into being by space salesmen. But where they have been most successful, it has usually been in fields where the old established magazine had lost some of its editorial vigor and the reins have been turned over to the salesman-publisher, too. Do a little homework on this, and it will be revealing to you.

Well, now, if we are to have editor-publishers of the kind that built some of the great magazines we are going to have to have a little different concept of the editor than we do in some cases today.

201

First of all, he is going to travel to beat hell. He is going to readers, to news sources and to advertisers. He is going to have to learn from the readers, learn from the news sources and educate the advertisers. This, you see, is quite a man.

There are quite a few such men around. But even those publications fortunate enough to have one such do very little about developing more of these total editors. After the top editor, there is a great tendency to leave the others at home. I am not persuaded that each succeeding crop of editors is as good as the one it follows.

I think this is because we have so many readership reports, and more dependable stringers, and better space salesmen, and stronger trade association staffs, and so the necessity for exposure of a large number of editors is becoming less all the time.

Now you will corner me afterwards and show me all the airline ticket stubs you have collected in the last year, and I can only say that I still think that more editorial people need more exposure to more of the publics that determine your success or failure.

Looking through two dozen serious magazines of all kinds last Sunday, I read the editorial pages, or the publisher's page, quickly looking for evidence of leadership. I guess my random sample was too random, because about all I got was an impression that in any area of specific interest, motherhood is still sacred.

When I was in college I worked on a daily newspaper and the editor of that paper wrote his own editorials. Sometimes they were on the first page, but usually on the editorial page. Sometimes there were three or four, but often there was only one. They had much to do with building a circulation far out of proportion to the significance of the paper, just as out in Emporia, Kansas, William Allen White did the same thing on an even more spectacular and more national basis. My editor's plan was simple: he looked around constantly asking himself, "What's wrong around here?"

and then wrote what he thought *was* wrong, and *who* should do something about it, or *what* should be done about it.

Probably I'm disappointing your program chairman by not keeping my talk more narrowly related to the advertiser, but, as I said at the start, I think it's false to assume that the editor should look different to the publisher, reader, advertiser or editor himself.

As an advertiser, I want to buy readership, and I know that only editorial creates readership.

I want to buy space in publications with breadth and depth and consistency.

I want to buy space in publications that sparkle with inviting captions, and beckon with imaginative illustrations.

I want to buy space in publications where my clients' customers clip the editorials just as often as they do the bingo cards.

I want to buy space in publications where the editorial objectives are clear and brief and are restated again and again and again by the space salesmen as the warm-up for any pitch.

I want to buy space in publications where the editor is eager to have me open the hood, and excited about the opportunity to describe to me how the engine is designed.

I want to buy space in publications where I can't buy editorial, and where I know no one else can either, and where I'm pretty sure that the readers are going to sense that no one can.

Circulation statements are not passé. We are embroiled in a 12-year battle now to make them more useful. But as the years go by, I am sure that space buying and space selling will start with editorial appraisal and that circulation evaluation will be more in the nature of confirmation of distribution, and in the matching of markets.

We are in a virgin country in this editorial evaluation, but it has great promise. Help us; guide us; and don't resent us. More particularly, help your sales force learn what it is you are doing, and why you are doing it.

The only risk you run in doing so is that as more and more of us come to learn that all advertising values start with editorial, and as more and more of us devote the time and effort to trying to buy on editorial performance, then, of course, your performance will have to be constantly good.

But, surely, you wouldn't want it any other way.

The Business Press

Although in recent years Marsteller Inc. diversified into many kinds of advertising, it continues to place more space in business, technical and professional publications than any other agency.

As a consequence, Bill Marsteller has been both a close friend and critic of the trade paper press. His aspirations for the trade press sometimes seemed to be higher than those of the publishing companies themselves, but without doubt, he, more than any individual over the last 20 years, has been consulted by business press publishers on the many subjects related to their customers and their readers.

Here are two typical talks before publishing organizations. The speech "Partners in Advertising Effectiveness" was made at the Annual Meeting of National Business Publications in 1962. "The Twilight of Tweedledum" was delivered at the Annual Meeting of Business Publications Audit in 1969 and is one of perhaps 20 speeches Bill Marsteller made on the problems of conflict and audits within the business press community. In fact, as Chairman of the Board of the Association of Industrial Advertisers, in 1947 he established the first committee to attempt to bring about comparability in circulation data.

PARTNERS IN ADVERTISING EFFECTIVENESS

There's a dreadful tradition in publishers' meetings that requires that the program committee always invite a few advertisers or agency men to come before them and give them unshirted hell.

And advertisers and agency people habitually seem to be willing to do this, fortified with the universal belief that it is easier to run someone else's business than their own.

I used to accept all such invitations, full of piety, and anxious to save you from yourselves. But maturity has set in.

The physical evidence of this maturity is especially evident to my tailor; the intellectual evidence is more obscure. However, I have concluded that since I see so many problems in the management of our own company and our own industry which need correction, it is just good manners not to be so critical of you.

I accepted this assignment for only two reasons: the first is that, like an old-fashioned space salesman, I was going to be in the neighborhood anyway, so I thought I would drop in; the second is that the subject I was asked to harangue you on is *"Partners* in Advertising Effectiveness."

That isn't a very jazzy title. It sounds like a cross between the Boy Scout oath and the New Frontier. Change the "advertising" to "research," or "engineering," or "management," and you have the same headline as advertisements you have been carrying for years, written and placed

207

by people who had no respect for advertising, and given circulation by publishers with limited concern about advertising or its effectiveness.

So although it's pompous and dull, it is really pretty close to what I should like to talk to you about while you wait for the female traffic on the first tee to clear up a bit.

First, I'd like to ask you to accept three fundamentals of business paper publishing. Actually, of all publishing, but let's not confuse the issue by milling around with consumer books. I have never been really sure who it is they consume.

The principles I offer you are basic.

1. A business magazine must have an easily defined and easily understood publishing concept, else it has no reason for being.
2. A business magazine exists for the reader, not for the advertiser or the publisher.
3. Advertising must add interest and usefulness to the magazine, otherwise it should not be included.

As they used to say in Public Speaking I-A, let us examine each of these well-rounded precepts, one at a time.

"A business magazine must have an easily defined and easily understood publishing concept, else it has no reason for being."

This is the only one of my three points which is unilateral; the purpose of a publication rests with the publisher.

In our Agency, the media function is an important one. It is also simple and specific. The responsibility of our Media Department is to "match the client's communications objectives to the media which fulfill the most nearly compatible publishing objectives."

Quite clearly, therefore, our media people need two things before they start to work. They need, from the account group, the client objectives against which the advertising and sales promotion is being prepared. They need, from the publisher, similarly precise definition of what the

publication is trying to do, and to whom it is trying to do it.

Several years ago, as some of you will recall with irritation or discomfort, we asked the 136 business publications with which we were then placing the most business to please send us a simple statement of their publication objectives. It is not a new statistic that fewer than 30 per cent were able to give us a clear answer. Lest this sound like the one-sided carping I promised not to indulge in, let me also say that dozens of publishers told us that no buyer had ever before asked them for such an obvious media measurement.

And this failure to put a perimeter around your product is not unique to publishing. When we conduct what we call a "marketing audit" with a client, the first question we ask is, "What business are you in?" None of the subsequent questions in the interview ever cause such blank looks, frustration and executive buck-passing as this first, jarringly essential examination of business purpose.

What business are *you* in?

Publishing? So is *Playboy*.

Publishing to business management? So is the Department of Commerce.

What are you? How are you different? What is your aim? Unless you know, no one else will.

I commend to you, and to every space salesman in your employ, either the ANA or the National Industrial Conference Board studies on advertising effectiveness; hopefully, if you are serious about your business, both. They document so well the fact that the success or failure of advertising cannot be measured unless there are clear objectives against which to measure it.

All of us in business tend to measure success or failure in terms of sales or profit. But we must not confuse what they tell us. They are historic numbers. They are result, not cause. Most dangerous of all, they are static, while a business is dynamic.

Objectives can be applied against profits or sales, too, but it is folly for a company to set, let us say, an objective

of 20 per cent profit before taxes unless the product development and marketing objectives which precede it will support such fiscal attainment.

I think all too often we buy—and you sell—business paper space on trivialities. For example, the very idea that anyone would buy or sell business paper space on the basis of cost per thousand is incredible to me. I am annoyed by the illogic of the idea. Carried to its ultimate it can only mean buying more circulation than can be meaningful. Buying business paper space on the platform of cost per thousand can only lead to deliberate waste and reduced effectiveness for the advertiser, competition from other media, and editorial vacuity for the publisher.

How can we be so dumb? Only because we haven't thought hard enough about why there *are* business papers and what they are supposed to do, and finally, how each individual business paper must have a very individual reason for being alive.

The second writ I issued, under the authority vested in me by your program committee, said:

"A business magazine exists for the reader, not the advertiser or the publisher."

This comfortable commandment is useful to have around for the few remaining advertisers who think their presence carries a collateral right to a hunk of the editorial columns.

But it doesn't apply to any legitimate publisher or advertiser, does it?

Don't I wish!

The crime against which I now speak out is not so easily discernible as the old-fashioned exercise of muscle. And the guilty are not the clods who would deliberately pervert your publications. The guilty are nice, well-educated but self-centered people. Like you and me, for instance.

When we place an ad in *Mill & Factory* that ought to be in *Machine Design,* we help you edit for the advertiser, not the reader.

We send you a nice insert with a pop-up that gooses a

serious-minded reader of *Contractors & Engineers* in the nostrils when he turns the pages, and we have helped you take the business out of business publications.

We holler "BINGO!" and you pass out the corn and cards, figuring if it's good enough for the Catholic church, how much can it hurt publishing? I've got a friend who makes $150,000 a year and his hobby nowdays is tearing out all bingo, subscription and inquiry cards and sending them back blank. He likes the ones with air mail postage best. I get a wonderful warm feeling when I think about some of my publishing friends the day their mail room says, "Hey, boss, we got back 10,000 cards today, postage due, all blank." With the world so full of people ready to carry signs or sit in the street to protest something they don't understand, just think what dimensions a revolt against 100-pound stock could take!

Why don't you tell us to cut it out? Why don't *you* cut it out?

Why don't you say, loud and clear, "The most valuable thing I own is the trust and loyalty of my readers. I'll let you share that with me but I won't let you louse it up." The *New Yorker* does. *Scientific American* does. And they used to be desperately poor. But only in money; not in respect for their readers. They always treated their readers like, damn it, that's who they were working for. It is not accidental that both publications have remarkably devoted customers of both their circulation and advertising departments; so much so that you can't always get in without waiting.

I like new products and new literature departments, but I see a lot of retreads and hokum in these columns. You think the reader doesn't know? I see a lot of editing in these columns that fixes it so all the new products items come out the same length so that no one is short changed. Except the reader.

Several times I have been correctly quoted as saying I wish that all business publications were run by editors, not

211

guys who had been most successful in meeting their quotas. I say this in spite of the fact that some of my best friends *always* meet their quotas. I'd better quit saying it, of course, if I want to keep getting invited to the American plan-type deadfalls like this, instead of to Schrafft's, where the editors gather.

And I suppose I ought to say that there *are* exceptions—that a *few* ex-space salesmen make *great* publishers—so that each of you will not think that I'm talking about you. Anyway, you can *think* that.

But you see the editor grows up worrying only about the reader and he gets pretty evangelistic about looking after your most priceless asset: the reader. He understands that the only thing on God's Green Earth you have to sell—the only thing we have any moral right to spend our clients' money for—is a friendly, open-minded few minutes with some bird in Waxahatchie who wants to succeed in business and is really trying.

All this frantic racing around selling space and dreaming up fancy formulae to keep people from buying reminds me of the war-time story that went around when the Russians were pointing guns at Scandinavia and sardines were scarce.

There's this importer who calls a big food broker customer and says, "Look. I just got my hands on a shipment of a thousand cases of sardines. I paid $2,000 for them; you been a good customer, instead of spreading them around, I'll let you have them for $3,000."

Then the broker calls his biggest wholesaler and says, "Hey, Moe, you're in luck. I just got a line on a thousand cases of sardines, very special, very secret deal. They'll cost me $4,000; I'll let you have them for $5,000 on account you are my A-No. 1 customer."

So naturally he buys them. He calls a chain store buyer in Jersey and says, "Harry, I'm gonna do you a big favor. I just got my hands on a thousand cases of genuine Norwegian sardines, very black market, but for you I'll take the risk. They cost me $6,000; I'll let you have them for $7,000."

Harry buys. But he figures this is too good to let get away. So he calls his brother-in-law, who is a lawyer, and says, "Look; mostly I don't like you, but my sister married you, so I'm going to let you in on a deal, we should both make a nice dollar. I got my hands on a thousand cases of black market sardines for $10,000. Instead of putting them in the stores, you find a food broker who wants them for $12,000, we each make a $1,000."

So the brother-in-law calls his friend from Scarsdale who is a food broker and sells them for $15,000, giving his wife's relative $1,000. Only the food broker turned out to be the same one who bought the sardines from the importer in the first place. This time, he took a tin home for supper first, and they were spoiled. Next day he opened a hundred cans at random and they were all spoiled. So he called the importer.

"Look," he said. "These sardines you sold me. I sold them to a broker, he sold them to a wholesaler, he sold them to a chain, and now they come back to me because they're spoiled."

"Of course," the importer said. "They weren't for eating; they were for buying and selling."

Please don't forget; your magazines aren't for buying and selling—they're for reading.

Thus, the sermon progresses to the third beatitude:

"Advertising must add interest and usefulness to the business publication otherwise it should not be included."

If, in your lifetime, you put away enough mashed potatoes with publishers, you are bound to be offered the warming news that business paper readers plow through the magazines as much to read the advertising as the editorial.

If this has the slightest shred of truth—and I would consider you very wishy-washy to give up this lovely belief at this late date—then you must agree that junky, say-nothing advertising is just as bad for your property as junky, say-nothing editorial. It is, therefore, crummy editing to fill the

advertising pages with boring sheep-dip while buying booze for the editor who put zing into the spring issue.

Lest you think I am guilty of exaggeration, the text for this is a recent issue of *Purchasing* magazine. I do not wish to pick on this otherwise delightful publication; it just happened to be handy when I was doing the research for this talk. It is also pleasantly plump and therefore lends itself to quicker extrapolation. I quote:

"Overwhelming First Choice for Nearly 60 Years!"

You will not be surprised to find that this headline finishes with an exclamation point. It has a switchbox, inset in an award-ribbon, though the ribbon is yellow, not blue, and where I came from yellow was usually handed out for fourth place. But only an agency that had a competitive account would niggle.

A four-color insert: "A Tradition of Craftsmanship."

Next, a cat chasing a dog waiting for a man in the phone booth: "You can tell the SKF man by his complete line of bearings." What an image: In comes the SKF man and opens his case and there go those damn steel balls rolling all over the place!

Anyway, that's the image I had. I doubt if anyone else saw the ad.

Or this breath-snatcher: "Brubaker End Mills On the Moon?"

These are from the advertising pages. Come with me now to the editorial pages.

Lead article: "How to Negotiate."

Another: "No More Backdoor Selling at AP Parts."

And then over to new products, and I hope our account people are looking: "New Machine Screw Taps Own Holes," or "Heat Recirculator Reduces Fuel Bills."

Here you see the pox of business paper publishing: two editorial standards, with one in the administrative hands of agencies and advertisers who don't own the circulation lists and haven't the same understanding about why they must protect this asset. In this same issue of *Purchasing*

214

there is a Dow ad that is headed "Dow Aluminum for Railroads" and that is what the whole ad is about. The publisher won't like me, but I say it's the wrong audience and there are better publications for this ad. I wonder what would happen if the *Purchasing* lad in Detroit had gone back to that excellent agency in Bloomfield Hills and said, "This is a swell ad, but it belongs in *Modern Railroads.*" It would, I like to think, have resulted in one hell of a lot of business for *Purchasing* from MacManus, John & Adams over the next years.

I suspect that by now you are saying to yourselves, so what do *we* do about it?

That's the nicest thing about belonging to a club like this; you *can* do something about it. Even collectively; and the Department of Justice and the FTC will bless you for getting your collusive little heads together, just like union leaders or somebody who is outside the law.

You can do *lots* of things about it.

You can work with agencies and advertisers to run seminars on effectiveness in business paper advertising writing for agency and advertiser trainees. The present generation may be too old to save, but they're too preoccupied to stop their young people from doing a good job if the young people happen to know how.

You can run some media-buying seminars, not to prove that it isn't necessary for the subscriber to buy the book, but to prove that people read the book.

You can bring together typical readers in convenient locations and let your advertisers talk to them and ask them questions and see how they tick. You can invite your salesmen in, too; they'll learn at the same time.

You can search out the many fine, successful advertising campaigns in the business press and put them on slides and send them all over to hungry ad writers and promotion program planners.

You can take a stand against publishing fads, opportunism and faint-heartedness.

215

You can hire some competent advertising man to write you a bible on media promotion, a form of advertising which in general has all the sparkle of mildewed leather.

You could, while building a case against steadily mounting postage rates, build a case against steadily mounting reader apathy. The first will cut your profits; the second will in due course put you out of business.

You could stand up before God and advertisers and everybody and say, "Look, guys; bad advertising can't succeed, but good advertising can't fail." And unless you know that from personal experience, you could spend some of your own money on good advertising for your own product until you prove it to your satisfaction, as we have done, or if you can't prove it, then quit taking money under false pretenses.

You could do *that*.

And then—and perhaps only then—you could say, "Look, partner, we've got a hell of a thing going. We've got a communications instrument every other nation in the world would pay a fortune to have, full-blown and dynamic. It's just like a computer; it'll do all kinds of crazy things that you can't do any other way, if we program it right, you and I. Let's get on with it, before somebody short-circuits it."

Is it worth all the effort?

It is, if you believe, as I do, that this is the age of the communicator.

And it is, if you believe, as I do, that no communications instrument is quite so clear and quite so useful as a great business paper.

THE TWILIGHT OF TWEEDLEDUM

This bit of gall I am about to deliver myself of is also divided into three parts.

216

First, I want to talk about the Twenty Year War for Comparability and the Common Audit.

Then I want to talk about the rather depressing position of the business press today.

Finally, I will make some suggestions for Utopia.

You didn't come here for a history lesson, but I'd like to retrace what has happened over the last 25 years in the quest for audited comparability of business paper circulations. It won't take long because damn little has happened.

World War II ended with many new free or controlled circulation magazines and there was every evidence that a substantial number were here to stay. Some were hurting their old established paid competitors, mostly because they were offering much, much higher circulation numbers. But were the magazines really going to the people claimed?

It was hard to tell. Quite a few weren't audited at all and the rest were audited by the predecessor of BPA, the Controlled Circulation Audit, which wasn't very highly regarded.

In 1947, what is now the Association of Industrial Advertisers, pressured by both paid and free publishers on the one side and buyer members of the other, established its first Media Policies Committee, headed by Harold Wilt of J. Walter Thompson. By 1948, AIA, followed by both the American Association of Advertising Agencies and the Association of National Advertisers, had issued resolutions urging, in effect, that sellers and buyers of business paper space work out a common form of audit.

Now there were two issues implicit in this. One was that we were seeking uniformly high standards of auditing. As I said, there was doubt that CCA provided this. Also, from the start there was the other issue of presenting circulation data in a manner that made easy comparison possible. Without true comparability we are mired down in known but unusable numbers. If we can't form comparisons of two or more publications in the same field, then audits themselves lose much of their usefulness to us. If we can't get comparable breakdowns, then the only true comparisons

will be on total circulation, the very thing that publishers who have been impeding progress seem to fear most. The alternative, and a dreadful one for buyer and seller, is the proliferation of individually developed agency and advertiser circulation questionnaires.

By 1950, CCA had been converted to BPA. It was well started on a progressive campaign to tighten auditing standards, to verify request circulation, and audit paid as well as controlled, a program which with relatively little interference has gone steadily ahead, responsive to the buyer. It is obvious, of course, that BPA had all to gain and nothing to lose by so doing.

Meanwhile, the Audit Bureau of Circulation, apparently feeling it had all to lose and nothing to gain since it had all the big business papers, and everything else for that matter, pulled branches around the cave and went into deep slumber. Occasionally someone peeked out to see if the pickets had gone away and issued a non-committal statement on behalf of continued contemplation.

In 1959, fed up with inaction and dozens of fruitless meetings, the AIA Media Policies Committee with Harold Wilt back as chairman got a place for a major presentation of the problem at the annual convention. Once again the plea was repeated, with national buyer weight behind it, for the audit bureaus to get together on a common audit. At about the same time our agency introduced the concept of editorial evaluation, so that if we could only simplify the statistics, we could then get on with space buying on the more substantive issues of quality and reader acceptance.

By this time the paid and controlled sales associations, ABP and NBP, had reached hardened positions that made mediation most difficult even though their influence on ABC and BPA was supposed to be indirect at best. Space salesmen were pumped full of ideological rose juice about the issue of paid circulation vs. free circulation. The real issue of course, wasn't ideological at all. It was postage parity. The Potomac River was the DMZ, often breached. The U. S. post office was where the action was.

In 1964, AIA took the lead in forming the Media Com-

parability Council, manned by some of the best people in the business. Once again meetings were held. And held. And held.

More time went by. Finally, ABP and NBP were combined into the American Business Press. Many of the key members of each were publishing both paid and controlled magazines and the lunacy of supporting divisive organizations was increasingly apparent.

Many of us hoped the same thing would happen to ABC and BPA. In retrospect, that seems naïve, because by now business papers had lost all control of their fate in ABC. The newspapers, far superior in numbers and monolithic in outlook, had gained effective veto power in ABC, if indeed that hadn't been the way it always was. Ever fearful that there would be some diabolical intrigue between controlled circulation business publications and the shopping news in Springfield, Illinois or Yazoo, Mississippi, they have effectively blocked every move to bring ABC into modern times.

There was a time when ABC, had it chose, would have been the sole auditing organization for the business press. There was a later time when it could have, had it been cooperative, been the auditing organization for paid, with BPA the auditing organization for free, working in concert with single standards and single classifications.

It is my reluctant conclusion that time has run out. I have concluded that at least insofar as the business press is concerned, the ABC is a boring anachronism.

I believe that we have the right to get action now on comparability. While it has always been desirable, it is now imperative if we are to use computers for at least the housekeeping and estimating part of the buying function. If we wait for another miscarriage from ABC, by that time computers may be superseded. It's like the guy who flunked the hearing test. He seated himself in the soundproof room, took his time getting settled and adjusted and finally said to the Doctor, "O.K., I'm ready," only to find out that the test was over.

It pains me to say this now, when I think the ABC di-

rectors are by far the most responsive they have been in my years of watching it. But the evidence seems to be that it is too late. There has already been mass defection from ABC. The business paper section is now a fairly unimportant segment of it. I suspect the newspapers, who have the most clout, wouldn't be unhappy to be shut of the problem.

For many years our agency has had a policy that no one from our company could serve on either ABC or BPA boards so that we could maintain neutrality and work for commonality of audit. Our Board dropped that policy this year because it no longer had relevance. We have come to the conclusion that we will be best served by a single auditing organization in the business paper field and that it is simply impossible any longer to hope that that might be the ABC.

Now a word about unaudited publications.

For 20 years, when someone has talked about the desirability of a common audit, the diversionary tactic has often been, "Yes, but how about all those unaudited books. Let's clean them up first." This has been said so often that some very intelligent people think there is something to it.

Both Bert Peller of J. Walter Thompson and Scotty Sawyer of our shop have done intensive independent analysis of the problem. Their conclusions are:

1. The hard core of unaudited publications is restricted to a very few fields.
2. The case of auditing needs to be strengthened as it applies to association and professional journals.
3. Many unaudited publications are directories associated with periodicals that *are* audited.
4. Except for these cases, unaudited publications get a very small percentage of advertising investment in business papers.

I think the best way to attack the unaudited publication is to have a strong, uniformly accepted single audit. Again and again when we ask why they aren't audited, their first response, however foolish, is that they don't want to get

220

caught in the crossfire, or they can't figure out which audit to join.

Of course, becoming obsessed with these mostly fly-by-night unaudited sheets is like swatting gnats when you are about to be devoured by alligators. The real problem for the good business papers is not bad business papers, but consumer magazines and television and the like, about which I'll have more to say in a minute.

In any event, lack of audit is a separate issue and I wish we could keep it to one side and deal with it separately. It has separate causes and separate cures.

For 25 years this ridiculous resistance movement against comparability or commonality has gone on and thousands upon thousands of hours have been lost in tail-chasing committees.

And meanwhile the big issue—the value and purpose and vitality of the business press—has gotten very little attention. With all the bickering over tweedledum and tweedle-dee, the industry has lacked a single, consistent voice to exploit the role of the business press. Even the merger of the old ABP and NBP was hedged with an understanding that the circulation issue would be declared out of bounds, impeding, I believe, fully effective promotion programs on behalf of the business press as a whole.

Harvey Conover, Sr., God rest his soul, told you years ago that the business press was going to be in bad competitive trouble with the general media unless it quit fighting itself and sold the institution instead.

It is clear that the prestige of the business press is as low as it has ever been. At a time when large industrial corporations are spending more and more money, less and less goes to the business press. Consumer media have moved in on the industrial market. Consumer advertising agencies have moved in on the industrial market. The counter efforts of the business press have not been distinguished, except in a few individual cases, and the nature and scope of business paper publishing is such that the problem cannot be solved by individual publications. There is crying need

for industry-wide programs to propagandize the business press for the great institution it is—while it is still a great institution.

When we talk to clients we hear things like, "Nobody reads the trade press any more." Does that annoy you as it does me? Often the man who says that has *Advertising Age* or *Datamation* or *Oil & Gas Journal* on the top of his pile of mail.

Another one we hear all the time is, "Business papers? We're using the *Wall Street Journal* and *Business Week*." One of the less bright things that this industry has done, I think, is to become ashamed of being called trade papers and go into this classy brainwash act to become business publications.

I read with regret the other day that *American Builder* had folded. I don't know all the reasons why, but it wasn't because we're running out of builders in America, or because they can't read any more, or because the building industry is collapsing. Any trade paper publisher, if I may be so bold as to call him that, ought to see some warning signals in that departure from among us.

I remain firmly convinced that the trade and professional and scientific press, at its best, is one of the most efficient communications alternatives available in today's society. For the advertisers whose products and services relate to it, it remains at the very top in a price-value ratio for advertising. Yet it gets a very small part of the credit, attention and revenue it deserves. It badly needs higher goals, more self-confidence, an improved image.

And how, pray tell, can this come about?

First, by speaking with a single confident voice. There exists a single promotion association; it will be strengthened if there is also a single auditing association.

Second, by ending the pettiness that has appalled, annoyed, or merely bored the buyer. Such things as the long-dead paid vs. free argument. Within a single audit, for instance, a buyer-czar could be appointed, classification by classification, to examine the comparability arguments and

then make a binding ruling so we can get on with other things. I see that BPA has a new staff position—manager of market comparability programs. If the purpose is to wet-nurse a new generation of meetings of publishers who will agree to any breakdown as long as they invented it, then God help us all. If, on the other hand, the plan is to hear everyone out, then make binding decisions, we have finally come of age. I am no longer impressed with "flexible" or "optional" comparability programs. At best, they needlessly delay progress; at worst, they are doomed to fail, the victim of natural self-interest. It's time to quit fooling around.

Third, accept the fact that association publications are here to stay and that all trade papers, technical papers, medical papers and so on are far more alike than different, and put a wing on the house to shelter the entire family.

Fourth, by massive and continuing industry-wide research into trade and professional paper reading habits that can be presented with all the real, live readers shown visually doing real, live reading.

Fifth, by teaching business paper buying techniques to the hundreds of new decision makers coming into the market every year.

Sixth, by moving rapidly into the new printing processes and the lavish use of editorial color, pictures and so on to compete with today's consumer media, not yesterday's trade papers.

Seventh, by a strong public relations campaign aimed at corporate management, marketing management and agency management.

Eighth, by opening much broader channels of communication between top publishing management and the true friends of the business press among both industrial and agency top management, so there will be updated readings on the operation and image of the business press.

And these are but a few. But notice how they nearly all —and I'll warrant nearly any you add to the list—depend upon the first: speak with a single strong voice.

To those of you who are deeply immersed in audit techniques I apologize for saying this, but that isn't the big apple. We have let ourselves get caught up in quarreling about techniques, and classifications, and methodology, and I say to hell with it. The real questions that must be answered are: Do people read the trade and professional press? Do the right people? How come they do? The emphasis in media research should shift from the *dimensions* of the medium to the *utility* of the medium.

As to the auditing associations, I think no matter what we do BPA is going to wind up with most of the players. It pretty much has. It probably ought to start acting right now like the war is over and it is the sole survivor, clean up the comparability issue in its own way quickly, and say to the publisher who can't or won't go along, "Enjoy yourself out there."

BPA ought to be sure it guards against the kind of problems that have so frustrated so many well intentioned people at ABC. It should put firm limits on tenure for directors, so that the board doesn't become a sort of phony club. It ought to be sure that neither paid nor free circulation can run things and write rules for competitive rather than auditing purposes. It ought to be tough as hell on audit violations. And it ought to be part of a total campaign to present the best case possible for the business press.

And that's what the rest of us should be doing, publishers of course, in the lead.

Unlike some of my associates, I am uncertain of the impact of electronics on the business press, over a long period of time. I am, however, convinced of the impact of piddling around with little issues and petty competition and entrenched positions. And if you aren't, look at the sad, steady decline in advertising page figures for business papers for the last decade.

I hope we're in the twilight days of tweedledum. I hope we can put our time against something more exciting and more rewarding. While it's still worth doing.

Education for Advertising Careers

When Bill Marsteller founded his advertising agency, one of his first steps was to employ Dr. Charles Sandage, Chairman of the Department of Advertising of the University of Illinois, as a consultant. Ever since, both Bill Marsteller and the agency have been deeply interested in advertising education. He has been a Director of the James Webb Young Fund for graduate education in advertising since its founding and through the years has appeared before many meetings of advertising educators, college students and high school students.

Two talks before such audiences give an insight into his views on advertising and advertising education. One, "The Significance of Advertising," was a speech before the 40th Annual Convention of the Illinois State High School Press Association, high school newspaper and yearbook editors and their teachers and advisors. The other, "A New Look at Advertising Education," was the principal speech at a nationwide symposium of advertisers, agencies, educators and graduate students honoring Dr. Sandage at the time of his retirement in May, 1968.

THE SIGNIFICANCE OF ADVERTISING

Exactly why I was asked to talk to you I'm not quite sure. Perhaps it is because I was once an editor of a high school newspaper right here in Champaign. Perhaps it is because I worked on the editorial staffs of daily newspapers in both a small town and a large city. Perhaps it is because I am product of the University of Illinois Journalism School. Perhaps it is because for some years now I have had a happy life in an advertising agency. But, actually, I expect the real reason I am on your program is because I was available.

I accepted this invitation to talk to you for two reasons. First of all, it is an opportunity and a challenge to meet with a group who are articulate leaders today, and who will without question supply leaders of tomorrow who will shape the thinking of others in businesses and communities all over the country. The second reason I accepted is that it would force me to do something I have wanted to do for a long time: to try to put into sequence my accumulating opinions about the significance and values and responsibilities of advertising in a free competitive economy.

Advertising is not a necessary commodity. It isn't needed to sustain existence. It isn't even very old. Depending upon what you mean by advertising, as a business it has been around for less than a hundred years, which in the span of history is barely more than a few minutes.

Like you men and women here, it's young, but doesn't like to be reminded of it; it has a good deal of know-how, but relatively little experience; it makes some mistakes, but has remarkable vitality to overcome them; it is enthusiastic, and often very charming, but sometimes a little thoughtless or ill-mannered; it has a long and promising life ahead of it—a life that can be full and profitable and useful and proud, or one that can slip into boredom and humdrum and self-seeking.

Some of you in this auditorium will undoubtedly find your life in advertising, and help determine what the future of this business—this dynamic communication force—will be.

Actually, advertising is already very close to you and your job as editors. Webster defines it as "a public notice." It came into being most of all as an information service. One simple fact of history shows how it performs this informational function, and what happens when it doesn't.

As you know, Elias Howe invented the sewing machine. What the history books overlook is that he couldn't get anyone to buy it. He was commercially so unsuccessful that he had to borrow a suit to go to his wife's funeral. He was ahead of his time, not with his invention, but because advertising wasn't understood. He had no understanding of how to explain the sewing machine to prospective buyers—there was no concept of advertising to tell its benefits in terms of labor saving and a better life, and it limped along with very little attention for years, so that after it had been invented, a whole generation of women lived and died without ever knowing it existed, and their lives and their families' lives were the more drab because there was no public notice of it.

Before your education is completed you will no doubt hear professors and teachers both praise and attack advertising.

Some will call it an economic waste; some will say that it raises prices; some will condemn it as misleading and deceitful; some will claim that it appeals to the lowest of

human emotions; and some will say that it is offensive to good taste, or simply boring.

On the other hand, it will be pointed out to you that advertising multiplies the sales of goods and services and, by expanding markets and creating demand where none existed, creates jobs and actually lowers prices. You will be told that it creates trust in companies and products, and therefore gives security for employees and investors. You will hear it described as a force necessary to keep consumption up to the constantly growing level of our productivity.

Like most sweeping statements in religion, politics, business or love, none of these claims is wholly true or wholly false. In some cases the claims should be judged against personal interests of the people who make them.

Does advertising lead or mislead? Do the editorial columns of a newspaper or a magazine, does the commentator on radio or television, lead or mislead?

It all depends. You as editors are sophisticated enough to know that one of your hardest jobs in writing a news story—even a simple report of how the Champaign High School football team beat Urbana (which they usually did when I was in school)—is to keep all the personal bias out of it. Did the head linesman really blow one when he called your left tackle offside, or is that what you wanted to see? When you start a report with the sentence, "Plans for the Senior Prom have finally been released by Charles Hudson, Chairman of the Committee," you have adroitly, though perhaps unwittingly, made it clear that Charlie Hudson has been goofing off, in your opinion.

By contrast, advertising is usually less misleading even than editorial, simply because it is recognized as self-seeking in the first place, and anyway it can't be misleading for very long, in the second place. Advertising, to be successful, must be truthful or it ceases to be read or believed, and at that point it ceases to be advertising.

James Webb Young, one of the leaders of modern advertising, says: "Advertising is a self-purifying stream; it is

229

out where you see it. What you do about what you read determines its success."

Deliberately misleading advertising amounts to only a small fraction of all advertising of any kind. Yet some does exist and is a ready target for critics. As Mr. Young says, it is out where you see it. It is far more difficult for the public to identify dishonesty in the practice of law or medicine or in the operation of a grocery store or an automobile agency, and yet enough cases come to light so that realistically we know that there are unscrupulous persons in all walks of life. There are laws and regulatory bodies to protect us against many abuses, and the Federal Trade Commission and the voluntary Better Business Bureau protect us against most advertising abuses, but the greatest protection is simply the hard light of constant exposure. Advertising always lives where all can see it; this is the most potent regulatory force that can be established.

Now, does advertising raise the cost of goods you buy, or does it lower them?

In the car you buy, perhaps more than $30 of the cost goes into advertising and you pay that cost. In the can of soup you buy, a fraction of a cent goes for advertising and you pay that cost. So in a sense, advertising does indeed raise prices.

But is this a real increase in price? Clearly, without advertising there would never have been a mass market for automobiles. Clearly, there would be no great assembly lines. An automobile would be built, one part at a time, assembled by hand. The car you buy would cost thousands of dollars more, and would be a luxury of only the very rich. You have only to look at some of the more underdeveloped countries of the world to substantiate this, and so the $30 per car for advertising is not really an added cost but a tremendous reduction in cost.

Then look at the other consequences of the mass marketing of automobiles—our filling stations, our automobile agencies, our network of roads so vital to the transportation of goods, to our enjoyment of life, and to our national se-

230

curity. Think of the vast number of jobs they all add to our economy.

What would happen if advertising stopped? It is hard to sense, yet there have been a few fortunately short-lived and local examples that can give us a taste.

A few years ago nearly all the newspapers of New York City were out on strike. The consequences went far beyond the people directly concerned with the newspaper business there, and far beyond the strange vacuum created by the unavailability of normal sources of news. Department store sales dropped 25 per cent. The sale of used cars came almost to a halt. Apartment rentals were nearly halved. Job applications fell. Even funeral attendance was off because there were no death notices. And the day the strike ended a national survey organization asked people, "What did you miss most about not having a newspaper?" Forty-two per cent answered, "Advertisements."

As editors, you may have already wished, or, if you continue in editorial work, you may someday wish that you could edit a publication without advertising. Wouldn't it be wonderful to have all that space to fill with pure editorial material?

There have been two significant attempts to operate great communication properties without advertising. In the magazine field, for many, many years, *The Reader's Digest* sold no advertising. Finally, rising costs of paper, printing, editorial material and distribution forced its owners to a hard decision: either the subscription and newsstand price must be raised substantially, which meant a far smaller number of people could buy it, or it had to take advertising. So you see, advertising can reduce prices in many ways. Today, of course, *The Reader's Digest* runs advertising, and is no less independent, no less interesting, and more widely distributed than it was before.

Most of you will not remember the ill-fated attempt to establish a newspaper in New York that would not carry advertising. It was the paper called *PM*, and it had unparalleled financial backing from a dedicated and wealthy

group of liberals headed by Marshall Field. The theory was that its pages would not be contaminated by commercialism; it would be undiluted by the sales messages of Macy's and Gimbel's and General Motors and the like. Millions of dollars went down the drain before this hard fact of publishing life was learned: advertising is part of what people buy when they buy a newspaper. People want to know about sales; people want to know about new merchandise. This is a form of information, and this, too, is a function of publishing.

Without advertising, our newspapers would be four or six pages, printed on cheap paper with poor, if any, illustrations. Our popular magazines would be virtually nonexistent. Trade and technical magazines would be few in number and sell for perhaps a $100 for a year's subscription.

Here is a wonderful commentary on the information function of advertising: one of today's most insidious critics of advertising is a man named Vance Packard. Not long ago he wrote a book called "Hidden Persuaders," which leveled a loaded attack on advertising. It became something of a best seller. But how did people get to know about it?

It was widely advertised in newspapers and magazines across the country. Advertising was the only way the publishers knew to sell a book attacking the means by which it was sold!

Advertising, it is said by its detractors, is offensive to good taste. The great growth of television has brought advertising into our homes in a highly personal way, and we in advertising have found ourselves with a powerful force we aren't always sure how to use. Programming is often juvenile, and commercials are sometimes irritating, or unpleasant, or are built around sales messages that make us a little squeamish.

Most of the problems arise around products which are personal in nature and not the subject of pleasant living room conversation. Take deodorants, for instance. It is a very delicate and difficult assignment to build tasteful ad-

vertising for deodorants. And yet, to say that we shouldn't advertise deodorants is highly questionable.

You are perhaps too young to remember what a city bus in the summer was like before Lifebuoy and Dial and Stopette, but I do, vividly. When your mother was your age, she didn't know what deodorant was. Some were on the market, sold in drug stores, hidden behind the counters and people were embarrassed to ask for them. No self-respecting man would use such a thing. Yet today, it is a tremendous market. Deodorants and deodorant soaps are everywhere, out on the counters, easily bought without shame or subterfuge, and a happy heat wave to all of you. This advertising did. Is it wrong?

How to introduce and sell such a product in good taste is not fully understood. There is a real challenge, and perhaps among you there are some answers or suggestions. If you have an original approach to this, you have a bright future in advertising.

The function of advertising in building security is not well understood. Really, only within the last fifteen years have companies used advertising for this purpose astutely.

In a speech, a few years ago, an executive of United States Steel summed it up with this statement: "I would rather own a market than a mill." What he had come to understand was that a new process for producing steel could make his multi-million dollar mill obsolete overnight, and the dollars that the thousands of ordinary people had invested in U.S. Steel stock would shrink in value. Thousands more would be out of jobs.

How can U.S. Steel hedge against this? There are two ways, not mutually exclusive. One is to keep up a constant program of research and development to continuously find new and better products, and new and better ways of making them. The second is to build such a strong and favorable image of U.S. Steel that customers will always want to do business with them. This is a job for advertising: to humanize the sometimes seemingly inhuman corporation; to explain its motives and its achievements and its aims; to

233

tell of its policies; to suggest uses for its products; to seek suggestions for new products and new markets.

This is the best possible hedge. Oversimplified, it means simply to build a large group of warm friends.

I grew up on the northwest side of Champaign. My father owned a neighborhood grocery store and when I was a boy there were no supermarkets. My father never advertised. Few grocery stores did. His customers lived within a few blocks of the store. He had no desire to get bigger; he didn't even know how.

In the late 1920's, the A & P, and National Tea and Kroger's came to town. Mind, there were prosperous years, but not for my father. For his customers took to reading the ads in the *Champaign News-Gazette* and going downtown to buy Ivory Soap and Maxwell House Coffee and other leading products. Gradually his business shrank, and finally it was sold out to a larger company. And so I lived first hand through a marketing revolution. When I was a boy, I helped in the store and scooped out bulk coffee—that was the only way it was sold—but supermarkets brought about packaged goods and advertising brought about supermarkets. Coffee was better; it was vacuum packed and fresh. Today, there is a far bigger selection of types and tastes. When I was a boy, I cut slices of cheese for customers from large loafs, and it wasn't awfully sanitary, and it was pretty inefficient, and the selection was limited. Today, I can pick out the cheese of my choice, neatly and cleanly packaged, with little wasted time, and with a big saving in manpower.

My father was the loser in this marketing revolution, and many like him have been caught up through the years in similar situations in nearly every type of distribution. In a sense, we could blame advertising for his failure in his business; but while he failed, thousands were able to buy better food, a far more interesting and palatable variety of food, and at lower prices than would otherwise be available.

We in advertising have a responsibility to make its power known to all kinds of business, large and small.

Bruce Barton has pointed out that advertising is the very essence of democracy. An election goes on every minute of every business day across the counters of hundreds of thousands of stores and shops where the customers state their preferences and determine which manufacturer and which product shall be the leader today, and which shall lead tomorrow. In this fair but fierce competition for public preference, he says, every manufacturer must strive through continuous research to improve his product.

And not incidentally, he says, what little advertising there is in totalitarian countries like Russia and Red China is rigidly controlled, and understandably so. Don't you see how dangerous it would be to let a captive people freely choose their food, their clothing, their tools or their homes? Such freedom could all too easily expand to the ultimate goal of choosing their leaders and their way of life.

In the advertising agency with which I am associated we also promote such non-consumer products as railroad locomotives, electronic computers, earth-moving equipment, and steel. What can advertising do for such products?

Well, advertising directed to railroad men and to the financial world that had to put up the money had much to do with ending the uneconomic tradition of the steam engine and replacing it with the far more efficient diesel locomotive. It overcame entrenched opposition to change.

Advertising now directed to businessmen is informing them of the changes and improvements in data calculators coming almost monthly to cut the time and drudgery of accounting and scientific computation.

Advertising for one of our clients in the earth-moving field has helped speed the building of roads, has led to shortcuts in construction that have at least partially compensated for mounting labor costs, and has shown the opportunities for upgrading our unskilled labor force from degrading lifting and hauling to better-paid machine operation.

Advertising for steel has suggested thousands of new uses for better life and more economical building, cooking,

shipping and storing, to mention only a few day-to-day activities.

Advertising has permitted mass communication. One night recently a Greek tragedy you have no doubt read, *Œdipus Rex,* was performed on television. In that one night, more people saw it than in all the performances put together, in all countries of the world, in all the 2,386 years since Sophocles wrote it.

Advertising since World War II has cut down on forest fires, increased the sale of government bonds, helped fight deterioration of our school system, encouraged kids not to quit school short of a full education, and many other things, through the non-profit, totally volunteer Advertising Council, in which advertising agencies give creative work without charge, and media give space and time free for public-service messages.

But apart from your possible direct interest in the future as editors of newspapers or magazines or other media, and your obvious interest as consumers, what can all this mean to you as high school editors?

I think there is a great opportunity for you now in the use of advertising. I think your papers can be made better and stronger and more potent through advertising.

Our businesses are coming more and more to understand the immediate, dynamic potential of our young people as buyers and as buying influences on their whole families. Instead of simply announcement ads in your papers, if you will go to the businesses of your community with pre-written advertising messages, in the language you and your friends talk, with due analysis of what interests you in products, I think you can double and treble the advertising you may carry, or might wish to carry.

I have seen a few isolated examples of how this can work. An ad written by a high school student for high school students is said to have started a buying spree on colored sweat shirts in Texas that cleaned out a store in a day.

An ad series, written in newsy, chatty style about "who

236

was there" after school in a confectionery, doubled its business.

These are but examples. The lesson is obvious, and the opportunities are limited only by your own imaginations.

In a speech like this, I guess there is supposed to be a closing in which you are told that your future lies ahead of you and that the challenges are great. I have no desire to preach or to promise. It is obvious that your future is ahead of you, but it always will be. Of course the challenges are great, whatever that may mean. But they always were and they always will be. You live in different times than your mothers and fathers, and your children will live in different times than you do. I am not a philosopher; only a one-time editor turned advertising man who has had a lot of fun being both.

It's an interesting life I have, and some of you will someday want to sample it too. It revolves around creative people, and people who write, or compose, or direct, or sell are often very stimulating people. They are likely to be outgoing, almost always articulate, and usually very much concerned about what is going on around them.

There are the people that make up advertising, and when you know them and live with them, you come to be very sure that advertising is indeed a good, and honest, and dynamic, and growing force. It will affect you all of your lives, and I hope you will understand and forgive its sins, when you see them, and remind yourself of the great good it does, and see it as a force which will make us a happier people, a better informed people, a better satisfied people, and therefore, a stronger nation and a greater constructive influence in the world.

A LOOK AT ADVERTISING EDUCATION

At the University of Illinois Symposium Honoring
Dr. Charles Sandage

The thesis I wish to advance this evening is not a popular one. Very few educators, outside the ranks of the teachers of advertising, accept it. That in itself ought to make it popular with business, but oddly it is not.

In short, I believe that the trend toward simply a broad cultural education as preparation for a career in communications is a bad trend.

That's my thesis, oversimplified. Now let's see if it has any substance.

So far as I am able to determine, the history of the teaching of advertising has followed a pattern not unlike the teaching of any other relatively narrow occupational specialty, except for the professions. It found favor particularly in the large tax-supported universities, especially the land grant colleges that were founded on a tradition of teaching agricultural and mechanical arts, and, by easy extrapolation, various other commercial specifics.

It tended to be housed in Colleges of Commerce or Schools of Journalism, usually the latter, and was often barely tolerated in either case.

It gained curriculum permanency, along with other untraditional courses, during the depression when even a Journalism School graduate was held to be more employable than a liberal arts major, who in those hard days was believed to have learned nothing practical and to be marked with the additional stigma of not knowing what he wanted out of life.

The depression was almost a trade school climate. Benign conditions resulted in the proliferation of embarrassingly narrow, craft-oriented courses often taught by unprepared tutors who were more weedy than tweedy.

238

On this period I can be autobiographical. The University of Illinois was regarded then, as it is now, as one of the half-dozen best in the land for an education in advertising and communications. I graduated from the School of Journalism with a B.S. (Before Sandage) as an editorial major and an advertising minor with a fairly typical record. Among other credentials were these:

I had quite high grades, not too surprisingly since in three courses I was paid 40 cents an hour by the National Youth Administration to grade papers while taking the course.

I had credit hours in several exceptional fields, including newspaper morgue keeping, current events, and advertising layout, which turned out to be house organ layout because the man who taught it had never done anything else.

I had gotten through my last two years without owning, renting or borrowing a textbook of any kind.

I had a job on a local newspaper where a man who taught me a course in advertising copy five days a week worked for me on a copy desk on Saturday.

Now as I say, the University of Illinois was one of the best. In some schools, things were a little sloppy and unprofessional.

Seriously, advertising education everywhere was a pastepot and scissors kind of operation. It is not surprising that it was often scorned by responsible educators, and by men like me who more or less wasted college years in nontaxing exposure to corners and pieces of what is a very real, very rewarding and very sophisticated wide world of communications.

Now we have had a wide swing. It has become popular to declare that the universities must only give the cultural base to which industry will, on the job, add the craft competence.

This assumes several things:

First, that the advertising industry is equipped to teach

craft competence on a broad enough basis to support its personnel needs.

Second, that industry can (and indeed is willing to) teach anything that the university can.

And third, that the university's teaching probably won't be as good as industry can provide.

I think all three assumptions are false.

It is becoming increasingly apparent that not as many as 50 advertisers and advertising agencies combined now have or are likely to have any kind of formal training programs. Of these, I am aware of only two advertisers and less than a dozen advertising agencies where the program is complete enough or long-running enough to develop any measurable degree of advertising expertise in more than one or two sub specialties. Since industry employment is growing at a rate far beyond the capacity of this limited training effort, advertisers and agencies are going to have to depend on others. Even the agency heads who have had intoxicating love affairs with the Harvard Business School or inexact facsimile thereof on the one hand or Swarthmore or whatever on the other, are sending their recruiters in increasing numbers to mingle with the advertising majors at Illinois, Missouri, Northwestern, Wisconsin, NYU and other such places, fouling things up for those of us who have known that that's where the action was all the time.

The second assumption—that industry can and is willing to teach what the university should is the area I'd like to deal with in a little depth.

There are four broad subjects that can and ought to be present in college advertising teaching programs, that are rarely to be found in industry training programs. They are the ethics, economics, aesthetics and social and commercial relationships of advertising. They are the kind of subject matter to be found in heavy doses in the teaching of the professions. Let us examine them individually.

First, ethics, and let's include not purely moral considerations, but the more subjective area of good taste.

Advertising has been under severe attack in recent years.

While a lot of the criticism has been irresponsible, there are uncomfortably many documented cases of misleading or dishonest advertising. There are other, and more arguable, cases of lapses in good taste. To protect itself, the industry has set up some laudable self-policing procedures and various government actions have put still further boundaries on what may or may not be done in advertising.

The fact is, though, that there is no generally accepted code of ethical procedures and probably none could be composed that would erase the problem for all times. The solution lies in the original conception and execution—with the advertiser and the agency, acting not as fuzzy corporate structures but as individual, creative, competitive people.

I firmly believe that morals, taste and responsibility are ingrained traits. Our standards are strongly influenced by environment—by exposure, by example and to a very high degree by the teaching process. I believe it is impossible for many men and women to create or approve a vulgar ad or a misleading ad, even were they to be ordered to, as it is impossible for some people to be boorish or to lie or to cheat.

This, clearly, is an area where the college should be able to make a contribution. It is also an area that is likely to be forever blank in the background of the man or woman who comes into advertising out of a purely liberal arts education. It is not enough to simply attain general standards of morality and taste; it is important to be subjected to the deliberate considerations of *advertising* morality and taste, just as it is important for the law student to be exposed to the careful examination of the ethical concepts of the law.

I believe that early and deeply rooted standards of practice are essential to the practitioner of any business or profession if he is to get pride and fulfillment out of his work, not just a living; if he is to be a responsible social and economic innovator, not merely an opportunist. Here, I think, is a clear challenge for the university.

Some of advertising's critics attack it not alone on grounds of morals or taste, but on charges of wastefulness

or economics. Its defense has not been handled uniformly well.

Its most vocal supporters, naturally, have been the men and women who live and work in the industry. Only a handful of qualified students and teachers have argued its case, because only a handful have had the time and purpose to make a penetrating study of its value and efficiency.

In the industry, there are many extraordinarily talented creative people who produce advertising that is persuasive, charming or disarming, yet are struck dumb when they are asked to succinctly explain the economic value of the advertising they create. It is not surprising. They have learned their craft, but they have learned little about how it came into being, why it has grown, and what it really means in a social sense. They are left to plead its case without benefit of prior debate.

By its very character the university has a clear role here. The interdisciplinary opportunities are obvious and present to a degree and in a diversity the student will never have again. But it is not enough, I think, to send the advertising student across campus to the various survey courses in economics, sociology, psychology and the like, and say that he now has the base. If he is to maximize his usefulness to his industry later on, this body of information needs to be brought together and applied to the specifics of advertising. This is a great opportunity for curriculum development in advertising.

Of course, in this area there is need for much more and much more enlightened research. Properly, most of the advertising research done by individual media, agencies or advertisers has been self-oriented. It is, in effect, product research. Very little pure research is going on into the validity of the premises on which advertising itself is based. It is axiomatic that stronger teaching programs in advertising will result in stronger basic research. Advanced teaching and advanced research embrace each other.

Let's look now at the area of aesthetics.

Advertising agencies know that if they point their college

242

recruiting efforts toward the student with demonstrated interest in writing and art, they will reduce hiring errors. The American Association of Advertising Agencies has studied successful men and women in the industry, and concluded that working on the college newspaper is, for instance, one point of high correlation among the best advertising people.

If you dig below this rudimentary conclusion, you find that the most successful advertising people, especially in a creative sense, are those that had the most rigorous writing demands put upon them at an early age. My observation, further, is that where the agency and advertiser training programs fall down most is in the creative and writing area. It is rare that industry makes a creative person out of someone who was not identified as creative before he began working for a living.

To be sure, writing courses are taught outside the advertising curriculum and should be, but the opportunity for concentration should be available to the student who has to write, write, write to be happy. Here, in writing labs, he can be taught the rules, perhaps to be broken later, but with understanding.

But there's much more to it than writing. There is an understanding of the relationship of the visual and verbal, the implantation of tolerance for differences in styles and techniques.

And finally, there is the need to develop a deep respect for clarity, for mood and for beauty. This is not easy to gain on the subway. Again, it suggests an array of courses outside of advertising, but it cries for the teacher who can pull it all together and instill pride in creative commercialism superbly well done.

The fourth of the areas I would assign to the college teaching of advertising is the relationship of advertising to the greater field of communication.

The danger in teaching advertising as a craft, either in industry or in college, is that it seems to become an end in itself when it really is an optional form of communication. When I was a young man the popular definition of adver-

243

tising was that it was salesmanship in print. That is a definition with blinders, even if you add the electronic media that have come along since then. Advertising is simply a form of communication. It can work in concert with or instead of or even in opposition to publicity and public relations, word of mouth, unsponsored observation, even such subtle communicators as smell and feel. Some of the best minds in advertising are making much of this. In our company, we talk total communications, and we will build programs to promote a company's products or enhance its reputation through a wide range of techniques, by no means all of which are media advertising.

It is no longer enough to know how advertising works; it is imperative to understand and be able to choose among the alternative routes of communication.

At the university this is, of course, being recognized, through the renaming of schools and colleges to group together the totality of the communication process. This is as it should be, and will work counter to the trend to simply turn out the liberal arts student for a life in advertising or its sister communications services. As the business of advertising becomes the business of communications the task of on-the-job training is compounded by the necessity to include more and more specialities. Few businesses will be able to keep training programs running long enough to cover the full spectrum.

It seems to me that the total evidence points strongly away from the path advertisers and agencies and our associations have been taking in our relationships with the university. We have promoted gifts to the business schools or to the generalist schools, often at the expense of department of advertising or the college of communications. We have tried to curry favor with economists and sociologists to whom advertising is unpalatable and then, come June, have hunted up the advertising professors for help in hiring their best students.

Dr. Charles Sandage can certainly testify to this. He has probably produced more successful and more responsible

advertising men than any teacher who ever lived. Certainly, he has developed more teachers of advertising than anyone else has ever done.

He founded the most successful and longest running industry-educator program in existence. He conceived the James Webb Young Fund for advanced students in advertising, and begged his way across the land for enough money to get it going until today it has become the most significant—nearly the only—advanced study program in advertising. He has quietly tried to get a research center started on the basics of advertising here at the University of Illinois, a concept that is bound to come to fulfillment sooner or later.

In fact, Sandy's biggest problem through the years has been that he was consistently ahead of his time. There is almost nothing I have said here that Sandy hasn't been saying for years, cornering advertising people at conventions and seminars, tugging at their sleeves, and suggesting that in Champaign-Urbana things were going on in advertising education that they ought to know about. What I have had to say is merely an observation on a fundamental Sandage philosophy.

These are frightening times. Of all of the manifestations of unrest and confusion, none is more disturbing than the widespread student rebellions, and none is closer to home for the group of people here.

I have had children in school at Berkeley and Columbia and I have listened to their versions and the versions of their classmates about what these protests really meant. Almost without exception, the student rebellions have been led by professional revolutionaries such as Mario Savio, Bettina Aptheker, Mark Rudd and others, some of whom are even second-generation revolutionaries.

The rebellions start around local causes and sometimes trivial causes, and yet they grow and ultimately some non-revolutionary young people get caught up in them.

For the most part, the students that I have talked to have little sympathy with the leadership, but they are not com-

pletely out of sympathy with root causes that seem to feed the riots. Their complaints have a lot to do with the growing alienation between teacher and student and between student and administration. They find themselves in cynical times taught by cynical teachers in a megauniversity. The human relationship between the student and teacher is missing. The teacher all too often rushes off to his other occupations the minute the lecture is over.

Our young people want leadership, and warmth, and interest, and human involvement. They want to be recognized as individuals. These times cry out for teachers like Dr. Sandage, for teachers who are interested in people as people and in ideals as well as ideas.

This is a significant time to be honoring a career like Sandy's. He is the personification of what our students so desperately want in a teacher.

That's why as Sandy walks among us today he seems a little taller than most of us.